# The Self-Builder's Guide To Project Management

Vince Holden

Published by Holden Management.

Cover Design by Holden Management

ISBN 13: 978-0-9934064-4-7 Paperback

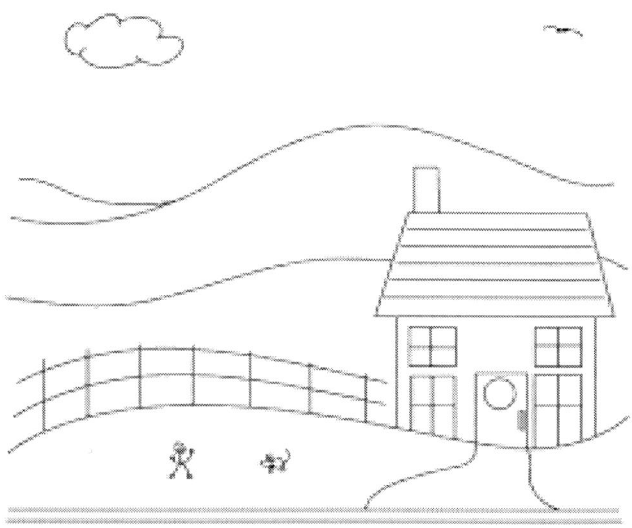

# About this Book

I decided to write this book for very similar reasons that I decided to follow the path to becoming a construction project manager rather than a building contractor. Quite simply, there is so much information required between the designer(s), client, and builder and too many gaps in the collation of this information.

I played the role of building contractor for many years, working with numerous architects, engineers, developers, private clients, Building Control, warranty surveyors, conservation officers, tradesmen, builders, merchants...the list is endless. But for almost as many years, I felt that all these ingredients lacked cohesion, relying upon the proficiency of the builder; his relationship with the client, architect, and other professionals; his want to try and bridge the gaps; a large portion of luck; and the dependence upon the making-it-up-as-you-go-along mantra. I filled those gaps, even though not really my role, and to the best of my knowledge, filled them very well.

However, not only do I consider myself a minority with this enthusiasm and knowledge, but as the scale of work increases from, say, extensions and modernisations, up through large re-furbs and new builds – so does the need for someone to glue it all together. This required management role escalates also with the inclusion of recent energy performance requirements, the coming (and going) of the Code for Sustainable Homes, ever-changing building regulations and planning policies, and most importantly, the thirst of Mr & Mrs Self-Build (SB) to build their own dream home with the inclusion of renewable technologies and low running costs.

Throw into the pot changing construction design management (CDM) – which encompasses all things health and safety – obligations, and numerous other legislations, it is no wonder that your average client and his building contractor rely more and more on independent knowledgeable input and guidance.

So that is where the project manager, or in this case, his book comes in.

I decided that there was a necessity for someplace that Mr & Mrs SB, wanting to manage their own project, could go to find lots of information and advice, and to learn about the many potential obstacles in the process, so that they could tackle their build process and supervision with their nerves intact.

**This book is just the place!**

Now, whilst it would take several volumes to try and cover literally every single possible aspect of construction management, I believe that I have addressed most elements to help you understand what is achievable, and how to ensure that the relevant boxes are ticked. Hopefully, with the aid of this book, your build stands a decent chance of arriving at its destination without crashing.

Building or re-furbishing your home is a huge task, and the amount of awareness required for this task is very often misunderstood and hugely underestimated. Therefore, using the following information and access to my knowledge base*, you will be in control with no nasty surprises, ensuring that you reach the end of your build with all your own hair intact and a project you are proud of.

** By buying this book, you are given exclusive rights to contact me for free expert advice on any of the subjects covered- see end of the book for details.*

# CONTENTS

# Part 1
## Introduction - The Concept

Knowledge Speaks
but
Wisdom Listens

# 1

# What do We Mean by a Self-Builder?

The self-build concept has existed in many forms for just about as long as construction work itself.

However, it is mainly in the past 10 years or so that Mr & Mrs SB have wanted to, and been practicably able to, become totally involved in the build process. We no longer need to buy a new house designed by others – built to a standard that could later prove to be questionable. We can now choose exactly what items are important, be it sustainability and renewable technology or the number and level of IT goodies. So, with the correct level of research and input at the design stage, as the self-builder, the world is your oyster.

It is not at all unusual for Mr SB to want to undertake certain small construction works, regardless of his skill level. Re-fitting a kitchen or – even with the help of tradesmen mates – building an extension is well within the boundaries of many people.

However, contemplating a major re-furb or building an entire house from scratch takes a totally different commitment, courage, and mind-set; and I am not referring to whether or not you can lay a brick or hang a door. This book is dedicated to the managerial skills required to organise the work and understand the importance of the correct procedures involved in self-building. You do not need Einstienesque thinking powers, nor is construction an exact science that you need to master; you simply need a relatively strong working understanding of the procedures, appropriate choices, and knowledge requirements of the project. There are tricks and there are also banana skins, but like most other things in this world, with the right information and guidance, you can develop the required skills.

This book will give even the most nervous first-timer correct and useful information to build their home.

There are fundamentally two different ways forward with self-building, and with it, two requirements to manage the process.

The simple way forward is to obtain your project, place all your preamble ducks in a row, then employ a builder as the main contractor to effectively take over from there. The amount of involvement from you towards the preambles is, of course, your choice. Some would prefer to simply employ an architectural practice to handle just about everything - from planning to handing over the keys at the end. But of course, this is not self-building and, without doubt, comes at a cost.

To an extent, the builder would assist with some elements of the pre-construction works for you and, therefore, the project management. Whilst technically this is still self-building, you are giving up control to the builder, and with it, the satisfaction of knowing that you created the end product.

A significant portion of this book is dedicated to the preambles, and so, to providing you with a valuable understanding of the workings of the management process. However, by deciding to use a building contractor, you are dramatically reducing your own input, and with it, the knowledge and control, both in terms of cost and specifications.

The second and most exciting way forward is to obtain the project, have a significant input in the design and execution of the pre-construction requirements, and then manage the whole construction phase yourself with sub-contractors till the end. This to me is the most invigorating way to self-build, but clearly, it is not for the faint-hearted. This way forward is where high competence with project management is absolutely essential, and you really do need to know your onions. You do not want to firefight your way through the project but, instead, carefully plan and manage each element with confidence and strength. I have over forty years of experience – you probably don't, otherwise you would not be reading this book – but it does not take all that time to understand, plan, and manage your build if you have the right tools at hand.

With the knowledge gleaned from this book, an investment of time, and the correct attitude, you will be able to see your project take shape right before your eyes, knowing that all bases are covered and that you have controlled as much as possible.

# 2

# What is a Project Manager in Construction?

What is a construction project manager? Can you do this yourself or do you need to outsource it?

By buying this book, you are indicating that you feel that this role is for you. However, this is a task easily underestimated, requiring at least a basic understanding of construction methods. But equally important is having the sense to realise that the majority of aspects involve professionals with many years of experience. The clever ones of you will know which professionals are needed and which are not.

## The Project Manager

Project management is the application of processes, methods, knowledge, skills and experience to achieve the project objectives. A project is a unique, transient endeavour, undertaken to achieve planned objectives, which could be defined in terms of outputs, outcomes or benefits.

To put it simply:
Project management entails making sure that the right person is in the right place, doing the right job, with the right materials, for the right cost, at the right time.

Let's explore this further.

**The right person**
If you were to make a list of all the people that you can think of, who would contribute to the project, then you would be surprised. However, this would be a good starting point and would assist you in numerous aspects, from programming down to costing.

The list begins with the architect, structural engineer, numerous surveyors – topographical, ecological, soil, and so on – through trade elements and tradesmen, and on to different salespersons like kitchen designers and wall tiling professionals.

**The right place**
This may seem the obvious one, namely the site itself, but it could also involve yourself at the architect's office or the kitchen showroom. What about trips to the builder's merchant to choose bricks?

**The right job**
This could mean ensuring that the correct works are included within the appropriate element within the schedule of works (we will get to that later) and, therefore, making the element cost effective.

For example, whilst building the foundation is in effect a bricklayer's job, it would not be practical to include it in the brickworks package, but in the groundworks package. However, if a bill of quantities were to be provided, it would show under brickworks.

The right job could also mean the obvious - do you want the carpenter to also be fixing the roof tiles? No, it is a separate trade with individual responsibilities and should remain so.

Likewise (and this is my pet subject), should the architect be providing project management? (See Chapter 6)

**The right materials**
Again, this may seem obvious. However, delving deeper than Is the studwork being built with 4" x 2" rather than CLS, which has a knock-on effect upon the door lining widths' would require a substantial understanding of all materials.

A lot of specifiers (quite often the architect) will specify generic materials found in their scheduling software. If I can give an example - I would welcome a £5 note for every time I saw a certain make of blocks specified by aforementioned specifier. Now, these are fine blocks providing all sorts of qualities; however, what most specifiers do not realise is that in the majority of cases, these blocks can only be bought in direct-to-site (full) loads and are rarely stocked on the shelf at merchants when your requirements do not fit the exact quantities of a full load. Equally performing blocks are readily available.

**The right cost**
Now, a perspective has to be established when calculating cost.

I am sure that you will appreciate the you-get-what-you-pay-for mantra. However, the cost of an item may not always be obvious - if you are able to source a cheaper material that is going to cost more to fix as opposed to the slightly costlier object that is easier (therefore, quicker; therefore, cheaper) to fix, then the cost takes on a different perspective.

Conversely, subject to geography, it is often advantageous to go looking for a sub-contractor outside your area to find a cheaper, equally proficient, price.

If you were to list all of the above, then multiply by the number of lists, the scope of your project management requirements would be staggering, but entirely necessary.

These are the fundamental building blocks (excuse the pun) of the entire project, and interlaced with one another, give just about any information required.

**The right time**

When a job suffers, probably the most likely culprit is the timings - one of the hardest to get right.

A programme of the works is an essential tool, but it is one that must be created realistically. The temptation would be to take at face value the stated duration of the individual trades; but you need to take in a pinch of slippage with each duration. Here's where the experienced manager has an advantage.

You still need a programme - no matter how basic or detailed -which not only tells you when each trader is due to commence or complete his section of the work, but also assists with any lead times (kitchen manufacture and installation ?) and cashflow forecast.

I usually create a programme on a spreadsheet with the trades down the left-hand side and the weeks across the top (see Chapter 23). The programme is relatively easy to adjust, if necessary, but it is best developed with a lot of thought to get it as near as right in the first place.

Start with all the preamble jobs – you will require electricity and water on-site before any works can commence, and this could take many months. A Section 80 demolition notice requires a minimum of 6 weeks to instigate before demo can commence; likewise, it takes several weeks to organise the disconnection of the existing services.

Here is an excerpt from an article that I wrote for my website, selling my services:

*The project manager will need to work with anyone involved in the build. This will include Building Control officers, conservation officers, and any other environmental representatives. They will also need to interact constantly with the design team to deal with any design issues or alterations which may occur.*

*The management of a construction project needs a particular set of skills. The project manager will need to carry out their duties appropriately and with enthusiasm. They must be able to motivate and yet maintain discipline. They need a variety of technical skills to be able to solve any problems when they occur and to keep the whole project rolling forward.*

*Programme management is essential to the smooth running of any project during the construction period. It can be carried out remotely, as long as there is someone on site who can provide all the required information. It is only with keeping a wary eye on everything though, that the build will continue to run smoothly.*

Unless you have many years' experience in construction - both in the mechanics and the management - there will be elements where you will require knowledgeable help.

Whether its knowing how to actually navigate the pre-construction process, or understanding the mechanism of the build and the sub-contractors, you will need that knowledge.

Now, I am not trying to discourage you from taking up this role; this book is aimed at providing you with practical advice, but part of that advice is, know your limitations. There may be aspects that you can happily tick yourself and there may be ones that you cannot. A good manager will delegate certain parts but will at least understand what they are.

Hopefully, by the time you have read this book, you will have filtered what you can do from what is beyond your capabilities. Or as an old friend of mine would say, 'Make sure it's your eyes that are wide open and not your mouth'!

Next comes site management.

Who is going to do this? Who will direct the day-to-day operations and how? If you aim to do it yourself, do you have the necessary technical experience? Do you have the required managerial skills and programme management know-how? Do you have the ability to act quickly and calmly when problems occur and panic abounds? Those are a lot of questions, and they all need answering if the project is to be a success. It's good being prepared in advance, but to maintain a healthy project is going to require the use of all of the aforementioned skills in the continuous reassessment of progress.

The site manager should knit the contractors' labour with the flow of materials. This keeps the whole project moving forward. The manager should also be able to motivate the labour force and develop a team spirit to make best use of everyone's talents and expertise. The manager must also be able to mediate between the various personalities in the team to ensure that friction is kept to a minimum. Managing a site is not about ordering people about and shouting, no matter how stressful the job may become. A cool, calm head needs to be maintained at all times. This, however, does not mean ignoring problems in the hope that they will go away. An attribute often underestimated is the necessary ability of a project manager to communicate with operatives at 'site level'.

The more time I spend project managing, especially with Mr & Mrs Self-Build, the more I realise that one of the biggest fears when you good people are contemplating embarking on the self-build journey is how to deal with 'the immortal subbie'.

At best, he (or occasionally she) is a know-it-all, pedantic prima donna who believes that the entire build hinges around his colossal ability – at worst, bitchy, argumentative, demanding, aggressive, and a downright pain in the backside!

This mind-set is not trade-specific; show me a self-employed tradesman, and I will show you the demigod of the construction industry, who single-handedly will want to dictate the programme of the complete works because everything must hinge around his artistry – when he's there, of course!

The situation is worsening by the ever-depleting stock of formally qualified trades and, in my opinion, is not going to improve any time soon, with so little new blood entering the industry.

I have been employing and managing subbies for over 35 years (I was one for quite a few); so I would like to think that I have dealt with all they have to offer. And believe me, it is an expert field in its own right, and not for the faint-hearted.

This brings me back to Mr & Mrs SB. They find the concept of building (or converting) their own dream home exciting. They have the plot, the funding, and the drawings, and dearly want to build using sub-contractors to keep the cost down. But, especially for first timers, the concept of spending most of the build on their knees at the whim of the plumber, bricky, or plasterer, with the programme torn up and the finished article rapidly retreating into the sunset, can make most good people contemplate pre-booking therapy sessions.

That's where the project manager comes in. His (or her) job is to choose the correct tradesman; once found, to programme, to manage and to wipe his brow - with builder speak; to point out fundamental ways towards a common goal - with builder speak; to show him that it's not his way or no way - with builder speak; to remind him of who's working for whom - with builder speak; and then to pat him on the head and send him on his way when his job is finished - with builder speak.

# 3

# What's in a Name?

I often ponder about what the best title for what I do for a living is. **Construction project manager** (CPM) is the closest to explaining it; but every architect, builder, and their dogs call their services 'project management', and to an extent, that is what they do.

However, whilst your average architect knows the procedures of, say, pre-commencement planning conditions, Building Regulations, service enquiries, and a whole load of spreadsheets and flow charts, does he know the nitty-gritty of building or how to deal with sub-contractors? No, probably not. Has he ever physically laid a brick to understand the correct consistency of mortar, planned the laying of a chipboard floor to minimise wastage, known the importance of having the materials dropped close to where they will be used? Of course not!

Then there is your building contractor. Clearly, he should know how to physically construct the building and deal with the subbies, but how much does he understand about modern sustainability and renewable technologies?

Does he do his own take-offs and understand cost control or does he simply employ a QS?

Does he know and appreciate CDM legislation and when (or not) to submit an F10 form to HSE? What does he understand about U-values, Robust details or SAP calcs?

To digress for a moment – whilst exhibiting at the recent Homebuilding & Renovating show at Epsom, an architect (project manager) came up to me and probed, 'What's the difference between what you offer and what I do?' Quick as a flash my foot soldier Fergie retorted, 'It's obvious, we know how to build a house and you don't!'That summed it all up for me.

Another time whilst at the show, two Yorkshire lads came to the stand to pick my brains.

'My mother-in law lives in an old house on a decent size plot and we are thinking of pulling it over and building a new house. Would we need permission?' one of the lads asked.

Fergie gave him an old-fashioned look and said, ' Yes, just out of courtesy, I think you should at least ask her before you do it!'

There was a moment's delay; then the penny dropped. Oh how we chuckled!

So, bearing in mind that I have taken it upon myself to study, experience, understand, and know all of the above and a whole lot more, I need a name to differentiate myself from other 'project managers'.

**C**onstruction **M**anager sounds like a glorified site agent (no offence).
**M**ission **M**anager sounds like I should work for NASA.
**C**onstruction **S**cheme **S**upervisor has a wishy-washy feel.
**C**onstruction **D**irector sounds too bossy.
**P**roject **A**dministrator is too removed and aloof.

You see? It's difficult to put across to my potential clients a name that they would recognise, yet sets me apart from hundreds of others out there claiming to offer what I can and do.

**Got it!** From now maybe I should call myself Vince Holden, **P**roject **L**eader and **A**dministrator of **N**eeds and **K**nowledge.

Mmmm, not sure about the acronym though.

I suppose I will have to stick to **CPM** then.

# 4

# Subbies or Building Contractors - Managing Expectations

Clearly there are two distinct ways of going about the build: one way is to employ individual sub-contractors and manage them, either by yourself or with the help of professionals; the other way is to employ a building contractor.

The main difference between the two, apart from the obvious cost benefit, is the way that you will need to manage your expectations.

"Seek to prevent disappointment by establishing in advance what can realistically be achieved or delivered, by a project, undertaking, course of action, and so on".

Now without getting too academic regarding the subject of project management, people who know how to manage expectations are able to more seamlessly navigate the choppy waters of their build. Why? Because they know how to communicate, organise, and direct conversations around getting things done, which is no mean feat when dealing with construction workers.

If you are effectively carving up the build into individual trade elements, you are at the same time multiplying the amount of communication requirements by the same number. Conversely, if you employ a building contractor, you only have to (in the main) understand and be understood by the boss / contracts manager of the one outfit. It is then his job to filter the information and pass it down through the workforce.

Now this might seem like a very basic and obvious subject, and if you naturally have communication and people skills, then the task should be straightforward. However, whilst YOU may think that you know what you are trying to build, do not take it for granted that the other people in the chain have received the thoughts in the way that you sent them.

People often get into hot water when they assume a tradesman, supplier, or even architect knows what people expect or even what they're talking about, so don't fall into the trap of assuming someone has the same understanding of a situation, project, deadline, or task that you do. You can avoid this pitfall by having a conversation in which you openly discuss what's expected, how it might be accomplished, and how success will be measured. Always leave plenty of opportunities for interaction, and remember that you are creating a team here where everyone has something to bring to the table.

One of the best ways to manage expectations is to make sure you communicate with everyone on a frequent basis. In the early stages of your project, at a key milestone, or as a deadline approaches, you may want to even *over*-communicate.

By holding frequent site meetings throughout the course of a project, you also have the chance to provide real-time status updates and discuss any delays, risks, or improvements. When you're proactively honest and transparent in your communication, you have room to put a plan B in place, if needed, or you have the flexibility of making new decisions as you move towards the finish line. Encouraging the tradesman or builder to be honest about a delay is a thousand times better than him making over-optimistic promises to deliver and then missing your deadline.

A huge aspect of managing expectations is the actual expectation, right?

You have to ensure that the expectations are realistic and achievable. If they're not, you can, and should, push back. The key here is pushing back in a way that balances the project's needs and the team's abilities. Being open about what can be delivered and what the plan is can go a long way towards instilling confidence and getting the job done. If you can nail the fine art of pushback, you've won half the battle of managing expectations successfully.

So taking on board all this science, the decision regarding the use of managed subbies versus a building contractor should not be taken lightly, and should be directly related to your capabilities to engage and manage.

I personally have no issues with all of the above or applying it to construction and the people doing it. However, I have been doing this for a long time, and I am used to dealing with whatever a build can throw at me, and the drama queens involved.

Don't get me wrong. I am sure that most of you reading this are just as capable of getting your point across. Just be aware as to how and how many times you may need to do it!

## What you should know when employing a builder under contract.

So you have decided the scope of works, found the builder at the right cost and are going to protect yourself by placing him under contract. In theory, this is all going in the right direction, but there are banana skins that you need to consider.

If you have specified everything completely, and are asking builder for a turn-key operation where he supplies everything, then to be fair the process should be reasonably straight forward. It's just a case of using the correct contract, and having a Contract Administrator in place. (unless using one of the small contracts for very minor works of say £25k ish)

However, if you are considering supplying certain items such as bathroom sanitryware, windows, wall tiles, or floor coverings for example, then you need to be careful, or else the contract has more holes in it than a trawler-man's fishing net.

For example:-

Lets say that you have agreed on 36 weeks for the works, with a penalty clause (liquidated damages) for running over time. You had better make sure that every "client supply" item hits the site bang on time; not too soon (I'll get to that in a minute) or too late, as it will no doubt effect the builder's programme and therefore place the job into client inflicted delays, with all manner of excuses and consequences.

And what about when the said sanitryware pitches up on site. Who is responsible for both accepting the product and keeping it safe? Builder?; maybe, but if he is not technically supplying it then he might not worry too much if your lovely bath get damaged before, during, or after it is fitted?

More importantly, at handover when you find that the bath is scratched, how can you hold builder responsible if he did not supply it as part of the contract works.

Whilst it sounds like a good idea for you to supply certain key items to save a few quid, the reality is that by the time you have written a myriad of caveats into the contract to protect against the above, the builder will apply costs at least the equivalent of any savings, so you might just as well include the items within his scope, but perhaps as nominated suppliers where you still specify/choose at an agreed cost, but he orders and supplies within his scope, therefore taking on liability for them.

One serious aspect of a contract that few people realise, regarding the agreed period for the works and agreed programme, needs to be borne in mind.

Imagine that you have agreed say 36 weeks for the works to be completed based on the programme as submitted and agreed. Then after 8 weeks, he is slipping behind programme, and by 15 weeks you know very well that he has more chance of becoming the next F1 world champion than completing your works on time.

In theory, and according to most standard contracts, you agree to the job taking (in this case) 36 weeks, and effectively turn the site over to the builder for this amount of time.

So even though you feel during this period that he is not performing as advertised, there is little you can do about it until he has actually NOT completed at the end of the agreed period, which is when technically the builder is in breach of the contract.

Of course this does not help you during the works when you know without doubt that you are heading for tears at bedtime, but can do little about it.

Now whilst there are clauses in standard contracts that address "Failure to proceed regularly and diligently"; to implement such a clause is both messy and requires very particular procedures along the way.

The secret is to not arrive at this position in the first place, by getting the correct advice: before, and during the build from an experienced Project Manager. (ahem)

# 5

# Who Bears the Risk?

I was in a meeting a while ago, discussing with a client the advantages of using managed sub-contractors over a main contractor, and the subject of risk came up.

I was asked that if, when using sub-contractors, there was no formal contract in place, such as a JCT, that was signed between a client and the building contractor, who would bear the risk if something went wrong?

The answer is - in ALL cases, the buck stops with the client if something goes wrong.

I was at the meeting because I had been invited to put together a team of sub-contracting tradesmen at relatively short notice because the main contractor who had previously secured the work had gone into liquidation the day before signing the contracts. I pointed out that the client was fortunate that the builder had not fallen over 2 weeks into the works rather instead of 2 weeks before, as they would have had quite a mess on their hands - contract or no contract.

In my opinion, a formal contract is little more than an agreement of procedure: it is not in any way a guarantee that the works will be completed and cannot possibly cater to the eventuality that the building company may be there one minute and not the next.

According to Builders' Merchant News, 48 builders go bust each week. Having been a main contractor for many years until 2010, I can empathise with the problems that come with being a builder, particularly in the climate of the past 10 years.

It is easy for the client to be seduced by the cheaper tendered quote or by the fact that the architect recommended or interviewed the builder. The reality is that information can be manipulated, and you have no real way of knowing whether or not the builder has purposely gone in cheap to 'buy' the job to help his cashflow. Likewise, how can you know that his sub-contractors (the ones that will help maintain his programme) are paid up to date. Yes, you can have credit checks done, but that only tells a small part of the story.

The way I see it, if you are employing individual sub-contractors managed by a project manager, then surely you are spreading the risk. Compartmentalising the works creates individual cells that only carry their own proportion of the threat. If a building contractor calls time, he is effectively taking all the trades with him, whether they like it or not, because they are employed by him and not the client.

However, by using managed sub-contractors, if one individual tradesman or supplier gets into trouble, of course it causes a problem; but it does not jeopardise the entire work.

# 6

# Choosing the Right Architect

You have probably gathered from earlier comments that I have rather specific views on the architect's role, and for the moment, we will use the word architect loosely to mean the person taking on the role. There are several levels of the architect's qualifications and skills, which we will explore a little further in the chapter.

The important aspect for you before deciding on the best architect is to first understand exactly what you want from them, which of course, is influenced largely by what you are building.

An architect has a role to play and is a commodity to be employed in just the same way as, say, a carpenter. However, as there are good and bad carpenters; so also there are good and not-so-good architects.

There is a lot of difference between the input required for a virgin plot of land with no planning yet, and a plot purchased with detailed planning ready to go, and whilst the majority of this book assumes the latter, to make my point, we will use the blank canvas of the former.

Take the case of you, the client, who have bought a plot of land, probably knowing that you will obtain some form of planning for your dream home. In that case, you need the services of a highly qualified architect. They will need to first understand the limitations of what you can build, and then go about designing it with you. A lot of skill and experience is required here, not only in the architectural sense but also in using the knowledge of the planning process.

However, if your project already has detailed planning approval and, therefore, only requires the mechanics of the build process to be put in place – Building Regulations, drawings, and so on – then a totally different level of expertise and qualification is needed and, therefore, a different level of expenditure from you.

And there is the crux of the matter: of course you can ask a highly qualified carpenter to put one shelf up, but you will no doubt pay for the privilege. Likewise, a large architectural practice will no doubt take on the job of obtaining your Building Regulations, but don't expect a small bill for the service.

Choosing your architect should take on a similar selection process as choosing the right plumber, including knowing exactly what their scope of work will be and gelling with their personality.

Now assuming that by reading this book you are hankering to project manage the works yourself, and you have read page by page, front to back, you will then be able to cherry pick the services required from your to-be-chosen architect. But a word of warning: the larger the architectural practice you go to, the more they will seduce you into needing their services. My cynicism on the architect's role is backed by many years of experience, both with construction mechanics and with the understanding of your average architect's capabilities.

If I can digress for a moment and give a small example: a while ago, I was invited to become involved in a project because the architect, who also boasted of project management services, was showing signs of – shall we say, not quite living up to expectations. Yes, he had designed a good-looking house where there had been outline planning to demolish the existing house and build another one in its place. The client, therefore, placed all his faith in the architect, and so, a path was set where because of the architect's whims regarding sustainability, certain aspects were designed into the house that proved to be first, beyond budget, but second, difficult to build physically. We brought the build back on track just before the start of the construction of what the client actually wanted, including his budget, rather than that of the architect. We also placed in order many other pre-construction aspects that were being ignored.

The focus had become the concept rather than the build, and this is sometimes where architects need reigning in.

Now I know that this is easy for me to say, but the point is, do not lose sight of who is working for whom, and contemplate just how easy for you this control may be when choosing the right architect. Ego is a very strong trait in this aspect, so understand right from the start that you may have certain differences of opinion that have to be ironed out <u>by you.</u>

Take along your ideas, know your budget and time scale, and see how the architect responds, but always be prepared to keep an open mind, since the most outstanding, workable designs tend to result from collaborative discussions. Conversely, never allow your designer to take over the project and dissuade you from features you have set your heart on and can afford. Be prepared to speak up if you don't like the preliminary sketches and to change your designer altogether if you feel unhappy in the early stages. By initially employing an architect / designer on a limited basis, you will be able to monitor progress and your relationship without committing yourself to a full service.

Be prepared, as later, you will be required to make lots of decisions -sometimes quickly; for example, where the socket should be to how the banister should look - in order not to slow down work on site.

Therefore, a relaxed level of communication between yourself and your architect is imperative.

So, unless you happen to be extremely confident in dealing with planners and grappling with Building Regulations, it is likely that you will call in a professional to help circumnavigate the red tape and bring out the best in your self-build project. Planning your new home should be the fun part, when all your dreams finally start to become reality, but finding the right designer can prove a headache, and you need to consider many important factors. Choose the wrong designer, and the home of your dreams can turn from grand into just plain bland, or it can end up costing far more than your initial budget.

Understanding the services and roles offered by various design professionals is the first stage to finding the right one for your particular project.

It is a sad fact that architects have gained a reputation for listening to a brief and then imposing their own tastes anyway. It is true to say that each individual will have his or her own preferences, style, and trademarks, so always try to find someone with experience in designing the kind of home you prefer, be it traditional or contemporary. Ask to see some recently completed properties of a scale similar to your own, and talk to former clients to learn about their impressions before committing.

Let's explore the different professionals who sit under the general umbrella of an 'architect'.

## Architects

One area of particular confusion is what actually constitutes an architect, with the term often used generically to describe almost anyone who designs or supervises the construction of buildings. In fact, the title is protected by law. A person is only allowed to call oneself an architect if professionally qualified and registered with the Architects Registration Board (ARB) following the usual seven years of training. The ARB is the authority established by statute to maintain a register of architects and to regulate the conduct of the architecture profession. Anyone calling themselves an architectural consultant or architectural designer has probably not completed this training and may have few qualifications at all.

Around 70 per cent of architects are chartered, which means they are members of the Royal Institute of British Architects (RIBA), which provides a free clients advisory service offering a database of all registered practices, including a profile of their work and the range of services they offer. All practices included in the register must hold professional indemnity insurance (PII) cover appropriate to the scale and type of work they undertake.

## Architectural Technologists

Like an architect, a fully qualified architectural technologist can undertake a building project from conception through to final certification, including the application of computer-aided design (CAD) techniques.

The term architectural technologist is actually quite new, and many still prefer to call themselves architectural technicians, despite a campaign to rebrand the profession and further raise its profile. This has established greater links between their education and training and that of architects.

Architectural technologists have their own professional body: the Chartered Institute of Architectural Technologists (CIAT), which publishes a directory of practices and ensures that members achieve approved standards of training, adhere to a code of conduct, and maintain PII. CIAT technologists currently need three years of supervised experience in addition to a first class degree, resulting in a total of six years of training.

Architectural technologists do offer design as part of their services but tend to specialise more in the technical aspects of building and the creation of the detailed drawings required.

The principal difference is that architects tend to place greater emphasis on conceptual design or how the house looks, whereas technologists are concerned with the technical performance of buildings and specifically draw upon science and technology in building design. Combine the two elements and, theoretically, you have the perfect solution. This is why so many architectural practices employ a technologist and vice versa. Often, it is the technologist who will prepare the detailed design and specifications, satisfying the legislative and regulatory requirements and solving technical problems once an architect has produced conceptual designs. However, bear in mind that only Chartered Architectural Technologists may practice on their own, while architectural technicians can only work in support roles.

### Surveyors

Chartered and technical surveyors are leading sources of advice on all aspects of land, property, construction, and the associated environmental issues. Many alterations, extensions, and new builds are planned by building surveyors who, if members of the Royal Institute of Chartered Surveyors (RICS), will be fully competent in matters of construction, and subject to the Institute's code of behaviour. Some 30 per cent of RICS members work in the construction industry with building surveyors managing projects from kitchen extensions to airport terminals, combining technical knowledge of construction methods and materials with legal, financial, design, and management skills.

The basic requirements for chartered surveyor status are a degree accredited by the RICS plus two years of structural training, followed by success in the RICS Assessment of Professional Competence. RICS rules lay down minimum levels of professional indemnity insurance for members in private practices.

## Package Designers

When considering self-building, another option is to approach some of the many companies offering complete self-build packages – from design through to supplying the materials and completing construction in either timber frame or brick and block. This can prove one of the easiest routes to self-build, with as much or little of the build co-ordinated for you. But beware of being limited to standard plans in order to keep the package competitively priced. It could be argued that a pre-designed kit will not best suit the individual requirements of either homeowners or sites, although some package companies do offer bespoke services to create a one-off property using their own in-house designer.

## Freelance Designers

It is worth remembering that a freelance designer does not need to be qualified to practice. There are good freelance designers who may prove to be cheaper options but will not necessarily carry the protection of indemnity insurance or be accepted by banks or building societies to certify for the release of funds. However, if you have your detailed planning approval and intend to project manage yourself but simply require Building Regulations submission and approval, it could be argued that hiring a freelance designer is a cost-effective way forward. Do your research to confirm these points.

## Plan Books and the Internet

It is not wise to use package companies, plan books, or internet-sourced designs to cannibalise as a free design service – you will technically be in breach of copyright. Even if a design is based on your own ideas, the copyright is owned by the individual or company that produced the actual physical plans, although referring to other house designs is a good way to become familiar with floor plans and gather information to achieve the best design for yourself.

On the subject of copyright and plans, some unscrupulous 'architects' who have produced drawings to get a scheme through planning may choose to charge a release fee for the design if you want to use the plans with a different professional moving forward.

## Interior Designers

Many interior design firms also act as project managers, co-ordinating architects and craftsmen, and may be ideally suited to a conversion or renovation project where they are working with an existing building that needs revamping. They often give free estimates and consultations and can save money by avoiding expensive mistakes with colour schemes and structural alterations. The Interior Decorators and Designers Association (IDDA) can provide names of members as well as additional guidance. Be warned, however, that there are a lot of amateurs out there. IDDA members are professionally trained and must comply with certain rules, including holding insurance cover. Thus it is wiser to hire IDDA professionals.

## DIY Design

A small number of self-builders opt to draw up their own plans, and, if you know exactly what you want and are confident in your abilities, you may decide to take this route. Building a scale model can prove a useful method of visualising the finished house. Software packages such as AutoCAD take the novice through tutorials that result in scale plans in 2D and 3D. The design is actually the easy bit; most people can orientate a building or work out a circulation route. But you will probably need professional help from a surveyor or engineer when it comes to the Building Regulations. Often, someone trained in design will see opportunities and avert potential disasters, which as a novice, you could miss. Be aware that if anything goes wrong with the construction as a result of your design, you will need PII to cover you. Additionally, most lenders stipulate that the design should be carried out by a professional holding PII.

If you are confident about your own building skills, you might simply need someone to prepare a set of drawings for submission to the planning authority. At the other end of the scale, you may prefer to employ someone who can help you through the whole process, from choosing a site to completion. An ideal setup would be a combination of people to produce the result: an architect to design the initial concept; the detailed design and specifications drawn up by the architectural technologist and an engineer; then, the entire scheme overseen by a project manager, with perhaps an interior designer brought in at the final stages. The inclusion of the project manager will avoid the blurring of who is responsible for each aspect of the project. Identify your needs and then match these to the professional who will be best suited to assist you.

## How Much Should You Pay?

Setting a budget for both the building and design aspects of your project and relating the size of a building to its ultimate cost is essential, whichever design route you choose. Although cutting costs at this stage may prove tempting, it really is a false economy. Your neighbour's father-in-law may offer inexpensive design services, but poor or inadequate drawings will incur additional costs on site and reduce the property's resale value; so it is important not to make too many cutbacks for such a vital part of the project. No one should begin work on the designs until you have first agreed to the basic fee, which will normally be quoted exclusive of VAT, expenses, and disbursements.

Routine work such as inspections or consultations is likely to be charged on an hourly basis; but for building projects where a full architectural service is provided, a percentage fee calculated on the total construction cost is usually suggested. With most design professionals, you should be able to select all or part of their services and, if you only want an hour's general advice, then that is all you should pay for. For a drawings-only service, some architects will charge by the hour.

Never pay for any design service upfront: a professional should be flexible and happy for the fee to be split into stages, with the normal arrangement for clients to pay by instalments on a monthly basis or at pre-defined RIBA stages. Often as with RICS members, there are no guidelines for fees. Rates vary depending on the nature of the scheme and the individual involved; and it is always worth negotiating the price.

Architectural fees for the full service should come to between 7.5 per cent and 16.5 per cent of the total building cost according to the scope of the work, although smaller practices with lower overheads tend to be cheaper.

Lump sum fees could be offered when the scope of work and budget can be clearly defined from the outset, with time-charged fees best chosen when these cannot be reasonably foreseen, as is often the case with repair or restoration work. It is advisable to visit several practices to discuss your requirements. Although initial consultations are free of charge from RIBA members, this may not be the case for all architects; so confirm fees before you meet.

For new work, an architectural technologist may charge a fixed fee, or a percentage of anything upwards of 5 per cent of construction costs. Although an architectural technologist is likely to be less expensive than an architect, don't expect a bargain basement price, as you can pay anything from a few hundred pounds for drawings to thousands for a full design and project management service, which should be broken down into stages. Where applicable, non-recoverable VAT is charged on a designer's fees and expenses. Although following the package company route could mean that you avoid paying VAT on the design service, as it would be incorporated into the complete package cost, be assured that there is no such thing as a free design.

## Contracts and Agreements

Having selected your architect, it is vital that a formal contract be written up along with a clear brief.

Governing bodies such as the Royal Institute of British Architects produce standard appointment documents from which you can select the precise services you need. Whoever you decide to employ as your designer, it is important that a contract is drawn up between you as, in law, without a specific arrangement, you may not have any comeback if your designer does not fulfil his or her obligations in some way. Always talk through any problems in the first instance.

However, as a last resort, you may have to initiate legal proceedings against them if things go wrong; therefore, a written agreement is the best form of a safety net.

In the event of a major structural defect, it will be possible to seek compensation from an inspecting professional, with most designers relying on professional indemnity insurance to settle any such claim. It is, therefore, vital to confirm that your chosen designer is sufficiently insured for the project.

## Making a Choice

Qualifications, however, are only half the story and, once you are satisfied that someone holds suitable credentials (by confirming membership of any relevant governing bodies or requesting a RIBA membership number), then it is time to talk. Compatibility and communication are vital, because when you start out on a project, the last thing you need is an architect you don't get along with or who doesn't listen to your ideas. Ask to see portfolios and visit any previously finished projects. But above all, talk, and choose someone you feel at ease with, communicate well with, and feel you can trust. Remember, you must feel totally confident in your chosen architect's creativity and ability to get things done. Bear in mind also that local architects / designers will have experience of the appropriate planning authority with whom they may have worked before.

For those setting out on the self-build road, thinking about hiring an architect will be high on the list of priorities. Will they be worth the added cost? What exactly will you get for your money? Even in the initial stages, talking to a professional can help get your project started, with many architects happy to advise on finding sites and to evaluate proposed plots prior to purchase. However, it is in the design and varied construction processes that architects really come into their own.

Having a good working relationship with your architect will give you peace of mind about your project and will ensure you get the end result you want.

Sometimes, however, problems emerge, relationships deteriorate, and people end up dismissing their architect halfway through a project (and even hiring another one).

The best guarantees of a good working relationship are:

- A really clear brief that sets out exactly what is expected.
- A good contract that sets out what happens if the project changes or problems arise.
- Absolute clarity on the fees, and how much you will be expected to pay when.
- Mutual respect and frequent communication throughout the project.

Architects are highly trained professionals who know far more about building and design than you do. But you are the client. Ultimately, the final say is yours, but you should respect their advice and suggestions. Architects usually take real pride in their work, and some can be quite resistant to doing things they don't like. But you are the one who has to live with it, and you should make sure you don't end up with something you regret.

**Choosing the design**

Once you have appointed an architect, he or she will draw up the plans for your project.

This should be an interactive process as you zero in on the final design. Ideally, they will produce several options and give you some choices, although usually the architect will make clear their preferences.

**Minimise the changes**

What often causes most stress in projects is the client changing their mind about what they want to do – or simply not making decisions.

Some changes are inevitable in big projects as they take shape, but any big changes will set the project back and add to the cost. So you should make sure you are clear about what you want before building work starts. Make as many decisions as possible before work starts on-site. The more the design is settled, the fewer unwelcome surprises there will be.

Should you get the architect to oversee the building work? Here is where my strong opinion kicks in.

Once you have the detailed plans, you could decide to use the architect to project manage, but unless they are very experienced at this, there are a number of reasons why it would normally be much easier and less fraught to have a professional project manager (PM) involved, or indeed, with the aid of this book, do the job yourself.

If the role is not for you, while it will cost a bit more, a PM will know all the pitfalls, and in particular, will not let the builder or architect take advantage of you.

Problems arise in all projects, and PMs are professional problem-solvers – it will be their problem, not yours (unless it is really big). They will help you through the numerous post-planning processes and deal with Building Control.

They should also put the construction work out to tender, getting quotes ideally from three different individual contractors, from which they will help you choose the most appropriate.

They will then handle the relationship with the builder on a day-to-day basis, ensuring that the work is done according to plan, that standards are maintained and short cuts avoided, and that it is completed on schedule and within budget.

Very few architects can do this.

# 7

# Types of Build Timber Frame, Masonry, or Other Systems

There are arguably, fundamentally two main methods of constructing the superstructure in the UK - masonry or traditional construction or timber frame construction.

In its basic form, masonry, which to some speaks for itself, usually involves an inner skin of blockwork and an outer skin of brick or blockwork. The two skins are separated by a cavity, which includes an element of insulation.

Timber fame construction usually has the inside skin constructed with an engineered timber-based panel, with the outer skin more often than not of brick or block. Again, there is a cavity that sometimes includes insulation.

The key difference between timber frame and masonry isn't so much the materials used to make the walls, but the fact that the timber frame is made in a factory and delivered to site in trucks.

This takes away a lot of the labour and simplifies the process from the builder's point of view. But brick and stone have been the favoured house building materials in Britain for the past 300 years, and this is what tends to make many people describe masonry as being 'traditional'. Both construction methods have their pros and cons, and it's not so much about which is better, as which is better for you.

## Price

For many years, masonry used to be thought of as slightly more expensive, but this is not necessarily true. The comparison is not down to the cost of the overall construction, but more that whilst similar in cost on paper, a timber frame can be constructed far more quickly, therefore making it cheaper when you take borrowing costs and other factors into consideration. The fact is that there really isn't that much of a cost difference. As a rule, masonry sits better (and cheaper) behind a brick or stone skin, whilst timber frame comes into its own with the ability to achieve far better insulation and airtightness values.

## Speed

Factory-produced homes are usually erected on-site in a time measured in days and have a clear advantage in terms of speed over traditional masonry construction. This is partly because the majority of the work to produce them has been done in a factory, and the actual work to construct them has started before the clock started ticking on-site. Once up, the internal finishes can be started right away, which can result in further time saving. However, bear in mind that thin-joint masonry promises many of the speed advantages of timber frame. This type of 'system' build gives the same result as traditional masonry but with the similar speed advantage of timber frame.

This can be achieved because thin-joint blockwork uses an adhesive rather than mortar, which means that far more blocks can be laid in one day than with a sand / cement mix. The inside skin is taken up independent of the external brick skin, including floors, and window openings are left in the same way as in timber frame. From the point of view of time spent building on-site, the thin-joint system is not far behind that of the timber frame.

### Accuracy

Timber frame construction tends to be a much more accurately engineered product. The walls are, therefore, usually straight and plumb, with the rooms kept square, unlike many site-built masonry homes. This can have advantages when it comes to fitting items like stairs and kitchen units. However, engineered houses require more accurate level foundations.

### Buildability

One of the main advantages of masonry is that all the items required are available at the local builders' merchant, and this is not the case with other systems. You can also be sure that all building workers will be familiar with masonry techniques. Timber frame though, involves cleaner, fairly straightforward carpentry skills, and the entire house comes on a lorry loaded (usually) with all the correct components, so further deliveries or trips down the merchant are not required. Usually, a dedicated, knowledgeable erecting crew used to working with timber frame would be the only labour required. With masonry, everything is built on-site, which can mean a lengthy duration to get the superstructure up. Brick and block is a 'wet' construction and needs time to dry out but, in particular, can't be laid in heavy rain or when it's below freezing.

In theory, subject to the hardiness of the labour, inclement weather would not have a significant effect on timber frame construction.

## Insurance and Selling On

There was once considerable prejudice against timber frame homes, but the fact is that timber frame has been used widely and successfully in North America and Scandinavia, not to mention Scotland, for decades, the stigma has now receded. Timber frame also has a slightly better warranty claims record than masonry. Consequently, timber frame is now accepted by all major lenders, insurers, and most homebuyers. There still appears to be a question mark raised by lenders, however, on the timber frame structure that does not have a brick or block outer skin but relies on carrier board based render system or other form of cladding fixed to the frame.

It is widely believed that a timber home will be more exposed to fire and subject to rot, but modern Building Regulations and the strict fireproofing of timber and dry lining means that fire is simply not an issue.

Rot and infestation are also not problems for timber frame homes, provided that the wood that gets wet is allowed to dry out properly and timber is treated with the proper stains and paints. Modern timber frames are pre-treated against many of the potential problems that blockwork lobbyists claim. Rot-producing fungi will only attack wood that has a moisture content consistently over 20 per cent. It's also worth noting that some of the world's oldest surviving structures are timber frame.

I spent my early carpentry years in the seventies working for a company that built 'Guildway' timber frame homes, which fundamentally are little different from their modern counterparts.

Here we are, 40 odd years later, with me still receiving advice queries about these buildings constructed during those years and still perfectly sound.

## Finance

Timber frame homes require a contract to be placed with a manufacturer some months before delivery. They also require a hefty deposit to be paid, putting a very different complexion on the cashflow, which may have to be accounted for in the way your mortgage is set up. The only comparable with masonry is any forward ordering necessary for bricks, which in the past year has required substantial lead times. Having said that, if orders for site materials are placed with a builder's merchant on a credit account, you would not be paying for materials until perhaps a month after receiving them on-site.

For the purpose of raising finance, brick and block can often be easier to finance with conventional lenders, as the stages mirror most self-build mortgage providers' stage payments. However, several lenders have tailored their lending criteria to suit timber frame construction, including the need for large deposits several weeks before any other works commence.

## Energy Efficiency

In theory, no system is inherently more energy efficient. It's all down to the design. In practice, a surprising amount of energy performance is also down to build quality and the materials that can be used. Simply put, the thicknesses of high-performance materials largely dictate the energy performance, and here, factory-built homes clearly win. It's also easier to fit insulation into timber frame walls and to leave the cavity between the two skins empty as well. It is far easier to produce better results in terms of insulation levels and airtightness with timber frame than masonry.

However, if we are leaning towards true passive house construction, the thermal mass of the internal block skin cannot easily be reproduced in timber frame.

### Noise

Heavyweight building techniques have a clear advantage here. But in detached housing, the chief area of concern is noise between floors, and most masonry homes actually have timber intermediate floors, so in this respect there is little difference.

## Masonry Construction

The issue of whether to build with masonry or timber frame is a hot topic in the self-build world, where a growing number of homes are built of timber frame, in contrast to mass housing, which is almost exclusively brick and block.

The difference lies in the fact that timber frame houses can be prefabricated off-site, which means that there are a large number of specialist timber frame manufacturers who cater directly to self-builders.

Yet, brick and block construction has several benefits. For a start, it offers higher levels of thermal mass and, when correctly insulated, can be almost as energy efficient as timber. It's also a well-understood system, meaning there is no shortage of builders or materials available locally. But perhaps most of all, advocates of masonry enjoy the inherent sense of solidity and soundproofing that the material offers.

## The Big Issues

- **Insulation:** With the exception of insulated concrete formwork (ICF), blockwork is typically insulated by means of creating a cavity, where a double skin of masonry (usually one of brickwork) sandwiches insulation. Due to recent changes to the building regulations, this cavity probably needs to be at least 125 mm wide.
- **Airtightness.** This is likely to be the biggest issue facing blockwork in the coming years – with the government pushing us towards building even more airtight homes – as masonry does not lend itself to an airtight structure as well as timber frame or structural insulated panels (SIPs). Simple measures can, however, be taken to increase airtightness, such as the use of special tapes and membranes.

## Option one: Aircrete

**Summary:** Lightweight blocks made by pressure cooking air into fine aggregate concrete have dominated the house building industry since the 1980s. Typical names include Thermalite or Celcon.

**Pros:** Aircrete is loved by brickies because they are easy to handle, easy to cut, and forgiving to lay. Because they are so light, they provide decent insulation and, therefore, can be used to help achieve lower U-values in walls.

**Cons:** Plasterers are not as fond of aircrete, as they report issues with movement and cracking. However, there are ways around this: one is to use plasterboard stuck on the walls (dot and dab), and there are modern wet plasters that will accommodate this.

**Option two: Thin joint system**

**Summary:** Uses aircrete blocks, but does away with the conventional 10 mm beds of cement mortar, instead using a 2-3 mm glue mortar, similar in characteristics to tile adhesive.

**Pros:** It sets very rapidly and, thus, enables blocklayers to use much larger blocks and to build them into walls much faster, thus saving on labour costs. When used wisely, it can add many of the benefits of off-site methods (timber frame), such as fast construction. It also helps achieve low airtightness levels.

**Cons:** The materials are more expensive, but this is offset by speed in the same way as timber frame.

**Option three: Concrete**

**Summary:** Traditional (pre-aircrete) concrete blockwork is still widely used. There are many manufacturers and lots of varieties of block, some denser than others, and most designed to be used in foundations.

**Pros:** It's slightly cheaper than aircrete and is often preferred in foundations and beam and block floors; also used where you want an exposed blockwork finish. It is also good for achieving high thermal mass.

**Cons:** It is slightly more labour-intensive to work with than aircrete and usually requires higher levels of insulation.

### Option four: Insulated concrete formwork

**Summary:** Insulated concrete formwork (ICF) systems are based around hollow polystyrene blocks, which are assembled into a wall before ready-mix concrete is poured into the hollow core. So, you start with the insulation and add the concrete later.

**Pros:** You get a super-insulated and airtight structure that's simple to build - indeed, some ICFs are designed to be built by unskilled labour. It works very well with rendered external finishes and can work out cheaper than traditional blockwork overall.

**Cons:** It can be expensive to add certain claddings to it, such as brickwork.

## Timber Frame Construction

Timber frame is extremely popular with self-builders, with over 22 per cent of all new homes using this method. However, the figure is slanted regionally, with more in Scotland, where it has long been a favourite.

In this method, the timber frame acts as a superstructure, supporting the entire building, so there's no need for internal load-bearing walls. The frame is prefabricated off-site in a factory, and there are several different methods of construction to choose from. Most manufacturers fabricate and erect the frame, taking it to the water-tight stage.

**Sustainability**

Timber from FSC sources is very eco-friendly – it's carbon-neutral, renewable, non-toxic, and organic, with a low embodied energy, especially if harvested locally.

**Speed Limits**

Take the matter of speed of construction. It has long been held that timber frame (built off-site) construction is quicker than blockwork (built on-site) for two reasons. One concerns the fact that because the frame is built off-site in a factory, the site work is simply a matter of erecting the frame, which takes just a few days. The other reason is that the frame is independent of the external wall cladding, so that once it is erected, work can then follow inside and outside simultaneously.

But the block makers came up with the thin-joint system, which not only speeds up the block laying process but also allows for the external claddings to be carried out independently, thus cancelling out much of the advantage of timber frame.

**Types of timber frame construction:**

**Open panel system**

This is timber frame in its basic form created by structural studwork and clad on the outside with a board material (plywood or OSB). Insulation of numerous forms, according to thermal levels, is inserted into the hollow frame panels, then covered with a vapour control layer (VCL) on the inside. Then, plasterboard and cables for wiring are run within the open panel of the frame. Different floor structures are installed, and, almost always, a trussed roof is used, but can be 'attic' trusses if rooms built in the roof space.

## Structural insulated panels

Many timber framers now prefer to use structural insulated panels (SIPs). The processes involved are similar to open panel – both are very much off-site systems – but SIPs come pre-insulated, thus enabling further speed savings and making it far easier to reach low U-values. An SIP is effectively a sandwich created with two sheets of (usually) OSB and pressure filled with PUR foam. There are no timber studs, but this sandwich creates a very strong structural panel that is fixed to the next with similarly made gussets. SIPs tend to be a little more expensive than open panel timber frame, but as the demands for ever-lower U-values continues, the cost differential narrows. SIPs are particularly apt when used to make open roof areas, as the roof can be laid as panels across supporting beams, therefore utilising more of the roof space. Since the inside surface is flat, internal battens are fixed to replicate 'studs' to fix the plasterboard to, and provide a void for cables and others.

Although there is nothing, in theory, to stop you putting a SIP roof on top of a masonry structure, it's something not widely practiced.

## Hybrid timber frame

At the time of writing this book, I am involved in the little-known hybrid timber frame system in the construction of a detached house.

It involves a twin wall of timber frame 300 mm wide, clad on the outside with board and an airtight membrane completely covering the inside. There is then the usual cavity with a brickwork outer leaf. The roof structure is a similar twin wall rafter and the floors are constructed in the same way as other timber frames.

The 300 mm void is then pressure blown with a cellulose-based insulation material, which provides significantly low U-values and airtightness. The whole thing sits on a passive concrete raft slab, and with the help of solar photovoltaic (PV) system, provides a SAP / EPC of A100; and that's just about as good as it gets!

### Quiet Floors

Many people steer away from timber frame because they assume that it will be noisy, and that sound will carry through walls and, particularly, through floors. In fact, a lot of self-builders choose masonry construction for no other reason than that it allows them to build with a precast concrete intermediate floor in order to keep the house quiet.

But you can get timber frame floors with a poured screed, which offers sound reduction every bit as good, if not better than, precast concrete. Liquid screed is designed to be pumped into timber floors, both as an acoustic barrier and as a medium for underfloor heating. The system has to be designed from the outset - it can't be installed as an afterthought - and it involves a layer of acoustic foam followed by high-density fibreboard under a layer of polythene sheeting. The anhydrite screed is then poured in a brief visit and left to set overnight. You can lay underfloor heating pipes within the screed, thus greatly simplifying the process.

### Thinner Walls

Whilst you can place any cladding against any background, some go better together than others.

Lightweight claddings – and this includes tiles and brick slips as well as weatherboarding – work incredibly well with framed constructions because you can fix them onto battening, which is itself fixed onto the subframe. Not only is this quick and easy to do, but it greatly reduces the width of the external wall. Instead of a typical 325 mm profile where brick or stone are used, you can build external walls at a thickness of just 225 mm. That's enough to increase your floor area by 4 per cent overall.

**Timber Frame – A Rising Sensation**

In recent history, almost all houses in the UK have been built from masonry blockwork – with timber frame, certainly in some areas, being seen as niche. This is with the exception of Scotland, which has always largely built with timber frame. However, in recent years, concrete's dominance has come under threat significantly from the rising popularity of timber frame construction and the rising cost of cement / aggregate products. Recently published statistics from the UK Timber Frame Association (UKTFA) are testament to this, reporting that the market share of timber frame has risen for the tenth year in a row. In Scotland, timber frame's market share is over 75 per cent and still rising.

The timber frame industry in the UK has continued to show its strength, resilience, and maturity despite these difficult times for homebuilding and the housing market. Timber frame is the right building solution for now and the future, as it has the ability to comply with and exceed current forthcoming building regulations and sustainability requirements.

Timber frame also performs better than any other building material in meeting the need to build sustainable homes, and the speed and efficiency of construction delivers the best economic solution.

**Making the Decision**

Most self-builders opting for blockwork will choose aircrete, with or without utilising the thin-joint system. Being lightweight, the blocks are far easier to lay, making it a popular system with bricklayers. However, that's not to say that dense concrete doesn't have its advantages – with designers looking to incorporate high levels of thermal mass, this is an ideal material that effectively allows the house to store and regulate internal heat.

If you are hoping to be more heavily involved on a DIY basis, ICF might be the system for you, as it is fairly simple to construct walls before the concrete is poured. Additionally, there's no need to buy additional wall insulation, and it's a lot more airtight than traditional masonry. However, this is not the system build for the novice.

Whichever method you choose to build, be sure to educate yourself on the ever-changing energy performance requirements, and if the quest for the ultimate in low carbon footprint is your criteria, I think you will find that timber frame will make the task easier and cheaper to achieve.

# Part 2
## Aspects of Pre-Construction

You don't know
what
You don't know

# 8

# Pre-Commencement Planning Conditions

There is a requirement to have the sometimes numerous planning conditions discharged. Any pre-commence conditions have to be submitted for discharge, and agreed before works can commence. If you are not employing a project manager (PM), then often, the architect will take care of this.

So let's assume that you have your plot and have planning approval. We will explore some of the more common pre-commence conditions and discuss some examples.

Most planning approvals will come with conditions, some of which must be satisfied before works commence, and others before occupation.

The pre-commence conditions will require an application to have the condition(s) discharged, and there will be a fee to pay for the privilege. The fee is per application, but several conditions can be applied for discharge in one application. The sense, therefore, is to collate several conditions under one application to keep the cost down.

Now, quite a lot of the information required to satisfy the conditions would have been integrated in the design and access statement, which would have accompanied the planning application in the first place, so it is a worthwhile exercise getting your hands on a copy if you did not initiate the application. This and other accompanying documents can be found on the planning portal or through the planning applications section on the local authority website.

Satisfying planning conditions can have a serious impact on the design and, therefore, the cost of the build, so it is worthwhile investigating this aspect as early as possible.

An important point to note is that you should read very carefully the wording of the condition.

1. Almost always, the first condition is in reference to the commencement date and speaks for itself:

**The development hereby permitted shall be commenced within three years from the date of this permission.**
**<u>Reason</u>: To accord with the provisions of Section 91 of the Town and Country Planning Act 1990 (as ammended)**

However, it is not unusual to take ownership of the site with this date close to running out, so for obvious reasons, there could be a bit of a hurry to get cracking and satisfy this most important condition.

I have been involved in many a site where it was necessary to, say, demolish an existing structure or even dig and concrete a small section of foundation to determine that the works have commenced, whilst other design works were still works in progress.

If this is the case, you will need to demonstrate in some way that you have commenced. The most common way is to involve Building Control by either submitting a demolition notice Section 80 (see Notices) or having the excavated trench inspected.

I recently had a client who mistakenly believed that by making his Section 106 agreement payment, he had demonstrated commencement. It did not, so we had to demolish the garage which formed part of the approval and did not in itself require a Section 80, therefore commencing works with only weeks to spare, whilst all other elements were put in place.

2. Usually, the second condition relates to materials to be used. Note the difference in the two examples:

**The materials to be used on the external serfaces of the development shall match those of the existing building unless first otherwise agreed in writing by the Local Planning Authority. The development shall be carried out and maintained in accordance with the approved details.**
**<u>Reason</u>: In the interest of the visual ameneties of the area.**
**Relevant policies – Local Plan DG1.**

Or;

**No development shall take place until details of the materials to be used in the construction of the external surfaces of the development hereby permitted shall have been submitted to and approved in writing by the local planning authority. Development shall be carried out in accordance with the approved details.**

Notice that the first one is a condition simply giving information to conform, whereas the second one is actually a pre-commence condition requiring approval.

They both relate to a new dwelling that had an existing house, which had obtained planning for a dwelling in the rear garden.

In both cases, they are referring to the materials to be used to construct the superstructure: face bricks, roof tiles, window and door design and material, any other distinguishing features like stonework or render colours.

Only in the second one are the planners insisting that an agreement be in place and in writing before works can commence. The first one would only be deemed not satisfied if say you chose to use a red brick for the new build and the existing house was rendered.

3. The requirement to provide a scheme which has to be approved for the landscaping and boundary treatments is very common.

**No development shall take place untill full details of both hard and soft landscape works have been submitted to and approved in writing by the Local Planning Authority and these works shall be carried out as aproved within the first planting season following the substantial completion of the development and retained in accordance with the approved details. Details to be included in the submission shall include plant numbers, grades and densities, materials to be used in hard surfaced areas, service routes plotted on a plan showing any tree planting that is proposed/required and boundary treatment. If within a period of five years from the date of planting of any tree or shrub shown on the approved landscaping plan, that tree or shrub, or any tree or shrub planted in replacement for it, is removed or uprooted or destroyed or dies, or becomes seriously damaged or defective, another tree or shrub of the same species and size as that originally planted shall be planted**

**in the immediate vicinity unless the Local planning Authority gives its prior written consent to any variation.**
**Reason: To ensure a form of development that maintains and contributes positively to the character and appearance of the area. Relevant Policy – Local Plan DG1**

The condition speaks for itself in its requirements and the fact that it is pre-commencement.

I would usually employ the services of a landscaping consultant, who would provide a scheme and drawings showing all of the numerous plants, etc. Whilst the temptation is to perhaps do this yourself (and indeed you could with the correct knowledge), the exercise does not only require you to show the numerous plants required but the size, spacing, and planting instructions for the individual shrubs and trees. The aforementioned consultant would be expected to know the local landscape officer's requirements regarding the suitability and ecological provisions for the different plants.

The scheme would also show any boundary fencing or walling along with hardscaping such as patios and pathways.

4. A not so common condition could be to take acoustic measures, as in the case of the following new-build that I was recently involved in, to be built near the flight path to Heathrow airport. A similar reason could be if you are building near a busy road or railway.

**No development shall take place until details of the measures to be taken to acoustically insulate all habitable rooms of the development against aircraft noise, together with the details of measures to provide ventilation to habitable rooms, have been submitted and approved in writing by the Local Planning Authority. The approved measures shall be carried out and completed before the development is first occupied for residential purposes and retained.**
**<u>Reason</u>: To ensure an acceptable living environment for future ocupiers. Relevant Policies Local Plan NAP2 H10**

As you can see, this is a pre-commence condition and would inevitably involve a specialist.

Quite a few ingredients of the dwelling fabric were affected by this condition - mainly the glazing to the windows. A noise survey was conducted with an extremely complicated formula being applied to the results.

We had to increase the glazing spec, but it also had an impact on the construction fabric (internal skin block type and cavity insulation). Also, the roof tiles and pitch had an influence on the depth of roof space insulation.

We were already considering involving a mechanical ventilation and heat recovery (MVHR) system for other reasons, but this condition confirmed its need, as trickle vents in the windows could not be used to meet the acoustic requirements.

Then we have the sustainability measures conditions.

5. At the time of writing this book, the Code for Sustainable Homes, which is an environmental assessment method for rating and certifying the performance of new homes based on BRE Global's EcoHomes scheme, has been phased out. Whilst it is a government-owned national standard intended to encourage continuous improvement in sustainable homebuilding, it is being replaced with local authorities' individual planning documents, which are then referred to in the following condition:

**No development shall take place until details of sustainability measures have been submitted to and approved in writing by the Local Planning Authority. These details shall demonstrate how the development would be efficient in the use of energy, water and materials in accordance with the Royal Borough of Windsor & Maidenhead Sustainable Design & Construction Supplementary Planning Document. The development shall be**

**carried out and subsequently retained and maintained in accordance with the approved details.**
**<u>Reason</u>: To ensure that measures to make the development sustainable and efficient in the use of energy, water and materials are included in the development and to comply with the Royal Borough of Windsor & Maidenhead Sustainable Design & Construction Supplementary Planning Document.**

Again, satisfying this condition can have serious design and cost implications and, more often than not, can include renewable technologies such as solar panels.

In this case, we were building using timber frame construction, so the implementation of other basic measures, such as water butts and low energy lighting throughout, enabled us to satisfy this condition without the need for renewables.

However, this condition and its approval are not to be confused with the energy performance calculation (SAP) and its design implications, covered elsewhere in this book.

6. Almost hand in glove with the preceding condition is Lifetime Homes Standard:

**No part of the development shall commence until evidence to demonstrate compliance with the Lifetimes Homes standard and other details of how the development will provide for the needs of an ageing population have been submitted to and approved in writing by the Local Planning Authority. The approved measures shall be implemented prior to the first occupation of the development and retained as such.**
**<u>Reason</u>: To ensure that the development is suitable for future occupiers, and to comply with the requirements of the Planning for an Ageing Population SPD.**

Lifetime Homes Standards are details designed to incorporate certain criteria that can be universally applied into new homes at minimal cost.

Each design feature adds to the comfort and convenience of the home and supports the changing needs of individuals and families at different stages of life.

Quite a few of the criteria are included within building regulations but can influence the general space requirements within the dwelling. The design can incorporate the provision for the future of the dwelling rather than its use initially, such as providing adequate fixings in walls or ceilings for the inclusion of hoisting facilities later.

7. In many urban or built up areas you could find yourself requiring a Construction Method Statement – to demonstrate a plan in place mainly for the management of site vehicles and personnel in relation to the neighbouring roads and dwellings:

**Prior to the commencement of any works of demolition or construction a management plan showing how demolition and construction traffic, (including cranes), materials storage, facilities for operatives and vehicle parking and manoeuvring will be accommodated during the works period shall be submitted to and approved in writing by the Local Planning Authority. The plan shall be implemented and maintained for the duration of the works or as may be agreed in writing by the Local Planning Authority.**
**Reason: In the interest of highway safety and the free flow of traffic. Relevant Policies – Local Plan T5**

This will now be mainly be covered within the new Construction (Design and Management) (CDM) regulations brought into force in April 2015 and are covered later in this book.

The above represents just a snapshot of the works, preparation, and potential cost implications of this particular aspect, and if it is your intention to project manage the entire build, then clear knowledge of these and any others, which may be a condition of your planning approval, is imperative.

Pre-commence conditions are exactly that and must be discharged before works commence. The last thing you want is a visit from the local planning enforcement officer.

The conditions stating, say 'before occupation' usually refer to items that would evolve during the works, but still need to be adhered to. It is not uncommon for the 'looser' conditions to be let slip through the net, only to rear their heads at a later date when a buyer's solicitor does a local authority search.

# 9

# Building Regulations Drawings Design and Application

Quite often, Building Regulations (BR) drawings are created by the same architect who creates the planning drawings, since fundamentally, the same model is used for the Building Regulations application, but with a lot more detail and reference for the mechanics of the build.

Building Regulations set minimum standards for the design and construction of buildings to ensure the safety and health of people in or about those buildings. They also include requirements to ensure that fuel and power is conserved, and facilities are provided for people, including those with disabilities, to access and move around inside the buildings.

Building Regulations approval does *not* mean the same as obtaining planning permission for your work.

In the same way, being granted planning permission is not the same as taking action to ensure that the work complies with Building Regulations.

Building Regulations are legal requirements intended to achieve a minimum standard for building work. Whether the structure is a new build, extending or altering an existing building, or changing the way a building is used, you will normally need to seek Building Regulations approval.

Building Regulations apply to most types of buildings including domestic, commercial, and industrial buildings. They specifically relate to the technical aspects of construction and include structural stability, fire resistance, means of escape, disabled access, weather resistance, thermal insulation, and drainage.

The detailed requirements of Building Regulations in England and Wales are scheduled within separate headings(Parts) each designated by a letter, and covering aspects such as structure, fire safety, access, electrical, protection from falling, drainage, and so on

Whereas planning drawings show basically what the building will look like, Building Regulations' detailed drawings show how it should be built. The drawings will show details to satisfy the numerous Parts of the Building Regulations and form the basics of the Building Regulations application and subsequent approval.

The Building Regulations package will include any structural design by an engineer and will quite often be approved by Building Control with conditions. These conditions may include details to follow, such as the calculations for floor beams or roof trusses.

However, if a system build is to be used, for example, timber frame (TF), the TF company will provide their own structural design pack to be incorporated within the BR application and will usually come under the conditions heading since the TF package would often be completed after other works such as groundworks are underway.

A brief overview of the Parts of the Building Regulations is as follows:

### Approved Document A (Structural safety)

Part A of the Building Regulations covers the technical guidance that supports the requirements with respect to structural safety.This document looks at and explains all the regulations for the actual structure of a building in terms of ensuring that the foundations can cope with the "load" imposed by the structure above and that they will not collapse, that the actual ground is up to the job of supporting the foundations and structure and that it will not move or subside.

Also covered is disproportionate collapse – This section states that, within reason, a structure should remain standing in the event of an accident. As you might be thinking, an accident could cover a great many things and levels of "severity" so buildings and types of structure are broken down into "Consequence Classes".

To summarise, Approved Document A covers the following items:

- Building Structure
- Structural loading
- Ground movement potential
- Disproportionate collapse

## Approved Document B (Fire safety)

Document B is by far the largest of all the approved documents and when you consider what it covers, namely fire safety, you can understand why.

Unfortunately, fires do happen in both domestic and non-domestic buildings and when they do, the top priority is ensuring that anyone in them can get out quickly, easily and safely and this is the purpose of this document.

Due to the many areas that need to be covered for domestic properties (e.g. houses, flats etc....) and non-domestic buildings (e.g. offices, factories, warehouses etc....) Document B is broken down into two documents:

- Approved Document B Volume 1 Domestic Properties
- Approved Document B Volume 2 Non-Domestic Properties

Both volumes cover essentially the same items, but obviously for two different scenarios such as means of fire warning and escape, internal fire spread for both the building's lining and its structure, the external spread of fire and also the access that is required by the fire services.

As a summary, Approved Document B (volumes one and two) cover:

- B1, means of warning and escape
- B2, internal fire spread for the buildings lining
- B3, Internal fire spread for the buildings structure
- B4, External fire spread

- Access and facilities required for the fire services

### Approved Document C (Resistance to contaminants and moisture)

The aim of this document is to set out the rules when it comes to preparing a site for construction works.

It should be ensured that vegetation or tree roots, topsoil or any pre-existing foundations do not affect the new foundations and their stability.

In the event that construction is taking place on ground that has been confirmed as contaminated, these contaminants need to be either removed or controlled so that they do not pose a health and safety risk.

Drainage (although also covered in Document H) is also a big consideration when it comes to the stability of foundations. Any ground moisture present needs to be controlled (e.g. using a DPC) and removed using suitable drainage pipes to prevent damage to foundations, walls and floors.

In summary, Approved Document C covers:

- Preparing a site and ensuring it is resistant to any contaminants
- Ensuring a site is resistant to moisture

### Approved Document D (Toxic substances)

Part D of the Building Regulations covers the technical

guidance that supports the requirements with respect to toxic substances.

In domestic projects, this would involve such matters as any underground gasses (methane or radon) that require control measures.

This is quite a short document and is mainly focused on cavity wall insulation and ensuring that any fumes produced by "Urea Formaldehyde" based foams are contained within the cavity area by a barrier and are prevented from entering the property so that they do not pose a health and safety risk to the occupants.

To summarise, Document D covers:

- Cavity insulation and preventing fumes from entering the property

## Approved Document E (Resistance to sound)

Part E of the Building Regulations covers the technical guidance that supports the requirements with respect to resistance to sound. This speaks for itself but involves both airborne and impact sound in say, the party wall of a pair of semi-detached houses or certain studwork walls within one dwelling. External influences could also involve aircraft noise or main roads. In terms of this document and a given building, it covers walls, ceilings, windows and floors.

Complaints about excess noise, or nuisance noise as it is known, is a major concern for most local authorities and councils and also for disputes between neighbours. Due to this, every property should be constructed in such a manner that any sound is kept within the given property space so that it does not disturb neighbour's or others within close proximity.

The types of building covered by the document include new buildings, material alterations to existing buildings, renovations of existing buildings, buildings that contain flats, buildings that are being split into flats and even properties that are created through a material change of use.

In summary, Approved Document E covers the following:

- Protection from unwanted sound from separate parts of a building and adjoining buildings
- Protection from sound within a house or home
- Reverberation that occurs within common internal areas of a building that contains flats or residential rooms
- The acoustic condition of school buildings and properties

## Approved Document F (Ventilation)

Part F of the Building Regulations covers the technical guidance that supports the requirements with respect to ventilation: adequate ventilation in roof spaces or cavities to avoid condensation, along with means of ventilation within the building in the form of extract to 'wet' areas or inclusion of MVHR. Like Document D, Document F is quite a short one.

The document states that there should be an suitable means of ventilation within a building, whether it's a domestic dwelling or place of work (non-dwelling).

In terms of ventilation in a domestic property, in most cases there are 3 main types – whole of building (ensuring air is continuously changed), extract ventilation (normally areas of humidity or pollution e.g. an extractor fan in a bathroom) and purge ventilation (depends on type of room and what needs to be extracted, may possible be as simple as opening a door or window!).

When it comes to non-domestic structures, the main aim is to make sure that air is continually circulated using items such as an air conditioning system, that potential issues with Legionnaire's disease are dealt with and that the system as a whole can be easily accessed and repaired.

As a summary, Approved Document F covers:

- Means of ventilation and air flow within a domestic or non-domestic building or structure

## Approved Document G (Sanitation, hot water safety, and water efficiency)

Part G the Building Regulations covers the technical guidance that supports the requirements with respect to sanitation, hot water safety, and water efficiency: adequate number of conveniences in bathrooms, separation of food preparation from sanitation, correct level of hot water storage and the adequacy of the storage vessel.

In general, Approved Document G aims to make sure that any drinking water provided is wholesome and drinkable (including softened water), water supplied to sinks, baths, showers and bidets should also be wholesome.

When it comes to efficiency, any means of supply including fittings and fixed appliances should use water in an efficient manner and avoid excess use or wastage.

In respect to hot water supplies, it should be ensured that any domestic dwelling that features a basin next to a food prep area, a shower, basin, bath or bidet in a bathroom or basin in a room next to a toilet should have a hot water supply

To summarise, Approved Document G covers the following areas:

- Supply of cold water
- Efficient use of water
- Supply of hot water and hot water systems
- Washing facilities and sanitary conveniences
- Bathrooms
- Food prep areas and kitchens

## Approved Document H (Drainage and waste disposal)

Approved Document H is kind of the next logical step on from Document G and looks at the drainage and waste disposal within and around a building including foul water, solid waste and rainwater drainage, the treatment of waste water and also separate drainage systems.

The document guidelines state that foul water needs to be drained to existing or private sewer, septic tank or cesspool and that these should be safe an not pose a health and safety risk, any rainwater needs to be drained away from the property correctly, any solid waste that is stored needs to be done in a safe manner and also any construction over or around a sewer.

The safe drainage or disposal of waste and foul water is essential to both the structure of a building and also the safety of its occupants and any issues with either of these could be potentially lethal to both a buildings structure and its inhabitants.

As a summary, Approved Document H covers the following points:

- Drainage of foul water
- Cesspools and wastewater treatment systems
- Drainage of rainwater
- Building and construction over and around sewers
- Separate drainage systems
- Storage of solid waste

## Approved Document J (Heat-producing appliances)

Part J of the Building Regulations covers the technical guidance that supports the requirements with respect to heat producing appliances. This covers the design and installation of primary and secondary heat sources, including flues and combustion. This document takes a look at the storage of fuel and combustion appliances and due to the nature of both of these items you can understand why these rules have to be in place.

On the whole, the document looks at the construction techniques and processes involved in ensuring that air is supplied in an adequate manner, combustion by-products (e.g. smoke, fumes etc....) are discharged correctly, the risk of carbon monoxide poisoning is managed, any fuel sources are stored correctly and pollution risks and sources are managed correctly.

When burning fuel (e.g. liquid fuel, solid fuel etc....) it is imperative that the appliance receives the correct amount of air so the fuel is burnt cleanly and it is equally important that any waste products are dispersed through the correct flue or chimney as if this is not done then the results can be fatal!

To summarise on the above, this document covers the following things:

- Supply of air
- Combustion by-product discharge and safe dispersal
- Carbon monoxide warning
- The protection of the building
- Providing correct and relevant information
- Correct protection of liquid fuel storage systems
- Protecting against pollution

## Approved Document K (Protection from falling)

Part K of the Building Regulations covers the technical guidance that supports the requirements with respect to protection from falling. This would involve the design and installation of stairs, handrails, balustrades, ramps and balconies, and includes access to basements. Particular types of glazing would fall into this part say a glass balustrade. With these points in mind, the rules aim to see that no one suffers injury from walking into open windows, ducts or skylights or gets trapped by others opening doors on to them. It also looks at making sure large panes of glass or glass doors can be identified as such, so that no one accidentally walks or runs into them.

If you are involved in a loft conversion or extension of some kind you may have come into contact with this document already as its other big focus is stairs and ensuring that they run within a certain pitch range, that their treads and risers are of a certain height and length and that they are generally safe and stable to use.

As a summary, this document covers the following areas:

- Protection from falling
- Protection from impact
- Protection from collision

### Approved Document L (Conservation of fuel and power)

Part L of the Building Regulations covers the technical guidance that supports the requirements with respect to conservation of fuel and power. This part, as it says, is about fuel usage, and its design requirements in the building. It can involve the heat loss (U-Value) calculation of the building fabric, the type of boiler and its efficiency, insulation requirements, and ventilation. As new technologies emerge, things need to change to reflect these new innovations and Document L is no different. To these ends it is split into four different documents, each focusing on a different area and age of building (either existing or new):

- L1A for power and fuel conservation in new dwelling building
- L1B for power and fuel conservation in existing dwelling buildings
- L2A for power and fuel conservation in non-dwelling new buildings
- L2B for power and fuel conservation in non-dwelling existing buildings

Overall, each document covers essentially the same topics but as technology and regulations change, such as the requirement to conserve more heat and power and reduce greenhouses gases and emissions, the rules in each document will need to change also.

For example, the insulation requirements of a new build property and what materials can be used may be vastly different from those that will need to be used in and older property undergoing renovation.

To summarise the content of these documents, they cover the following:

- Conserving heat and power in new and existing dwelling buildings
- Conserving heat and power in new and existing non-dwelling buildings

## Approved Document M (Access to and use of buildings)

Part M of the Building Regulations covers the technical guidance that support the requirements with respect to access to and use of buildings. This is mainly aimed at providing a building that can be used by people with mobility issues, such as those using wheelchairs, or people with impaired hearing or sight. It concerns access to and within the building as well as provisions for day-to-day use of sanitary conveniences and electrical sockets, switches, and so on. Access to a building or dwelling and then moving around inside is of paramount importance to the usefulness of the building itself and also for the comfort of those living, working or visiting it.

The basis of Document M is to ensure that accessing a property or structure is as easy as possible for both able bodies and non-able bodied users and once inside, they have access to any basic conveniences such as toilets and washrooms.

In some situations ramps and steps are needed to get to an entrance way and in these cases, this document sets out any required dimensions and degrees of pitch that these objects can run over along with heights and widths of stairs and corridors within the building itself.

As a summary, Document M covers the following areas:

- Accessing and using a building or dwelling
- Accessing extensions to buildings that are not dwellings
- Accessing sanitary conveniences in extensions to a building that is not a dwelling
- Accessing sanitary conveniences in a dwelling

## Approved Document N (Glazing safety)

*(Withdrawn on 6 April 2013 other than in Wales where it still applies).*

Part N of the Building Regulations covers the technical guidance that support the requirements with respect to glazing safety. This affects the heights and types of glazing requirements. As glass and glazing is present in pretty much all buildings, dwellings and structures you won't be surprised to learn that Document N exists specifically for this reason.

This document looks at the safety of glazing and protection against impact, ensures that glazing is obvious (e.g. making glass doors stand out) to anyone moving around a property, that windows, skylights and ventilation points can be opened and closed safely and that any glass or glazed surface can be accessed safely for cleaning.

As you may realize from above, there are some crossovers between this document and document K.

As an overview, Approved Document N covers the following areas:

- Protection against impact with glass and glazing
- Manifestation of glass and glazing within and around a property
- Ensuring windows, skylights and ventilation points open and close safely
- Accessing windows and glazing safely for cleaning

### Approved Document P (Electrical safety)

Part P of the Building Regulations covers the technical guidance that supports the requirements with respect to electrical safety. This is a very involved part which has many different electrical regulations for different applications – new build or renovation / extension. It is also the one that probably gets most attention out of all the Approved Documents – Approved Document P. This document itself is concerned with electrical safety and from a DIY perspective is hugely important as it discusses exactly what can be done and by who.

The main focus on this is competence and whether you are "competent" enough to carry out any works that you are allowed to do. In terms of the word "competent", this means that you have a full and competent knowledge of electrical installations and can check the safety of circuits and even issue a minor works certificate.

We all know the dangers involved with electricity and we all know to treat it with respect, so essentially, if you are not 110% sure on what you are doing, get a professional in!

To summarise, this document covers the following areas:

- The electrical safety in dwellings

## Approved Document Q (Security: Dwellings)

Part Q of the Building Regulations covers the technical guidance that supports the requirements with respect to the security of dwellings. It applies only to new dwellings and provides that reasonable provision must be made to resist unauthorised access to any dwelling; and any part of a building from which access can be gained to a flat within the building.

The document sets out reasonable standards for doors and windows to resist physical attack by a casual or opportunist burglar by being both sufficiently robust and fitted with appropriate hardware.

This Building Regulation applies to new homes and existing buildings that are being converted into new homes only (such as a warehouse, barn, etc). Existing homes are currently not required to meet the security requirements within Part Q.

**Approved Document R (electronic communications)**

The Government has published the Building Regulations Approved Document R introducing a new requirement for building physical infrastructure to facilitate high-speed electronic communications networks.

The new R1 requirement came into affect from 1st of January 2017 and means that all new buildings and existing buildings, which are subject to major renovation, must be equipped with a high-speed-ready, in-building physical infrastructure, up to a termination point for high-speed electronic communication networks.

A building will meet R1 so long as it is designed and constructed so that high-speed electronic communications networks can be installed in the future.

The requirement applies to both new dwellings and to buildings other than dwellings (except those buildings which are stated in the regulations as being exempt).

This new addition to the building regulations will mean that in future copper or fibre-optic cables or wireless devices capable of delivering broadband speeds of over 30 Mbps, can be installed into buildings.

## Approved Document 7: Materials and workmanship

Regulation 7 requires that building work is carried out:

- With adequate and proper materials which:
  1. Are appropriate for the circumstances in which they are used,
  2. Are adequately mixed or prepared, and
  3. Are applied, used or fixed so as adequately to perform the functions for which they are designed; and
- In a workmanlike manner.

# 10

# Building in a Conservation Area

If you are intending to build a new, or refurb an existing structure across a wide range of urban and rural UK locations, for example, in the historic centres of town and cities, it is entirely possible that you will come into contact with the term 'conservation area' when applying for planning approval.

In the United Kingdom, the term conservation area nearly always applies to an area (usually urban or the core of a village) considered worthy of preservation or enhancement because of its special architectural or historic interest.

In the current legislation in England and Wales, the Planning (Listed Buildings and Conservation Areas) Act 1990 (Section 69 and 70), defines the quality of a conservation area as being 'the character or appearance of which it is desirable to preserve or enhance'. The current Scottish legislation is the Planning (Listed Buildings and Conservation Areas) (Scotland) Act 1997.

In conservation areas, it is the protection of the quality and special interest of the neighbourhood or area as a whole that is intended, rather than specific buildings. For example, the layout of boundaries, roads, vistas, and viewpoints, trees and green features, street furniture and surfaces, the characteristic building materials of the area, the mix of different uses, and the design of shop fronts may all be taken into account when deciding whether an area has a particular special architectural or historic interest.

Therefore, whilst it is the role of the listed building process to protect individual buildings, it is common for many listed buildings to also be located within designated conservation areas where those individual buildings make a contribution to the special architectural or historic character of the area.

Current government planning policy on conservation areas is laid down (for England) mainly in Section 12, Conserving and Enhancing the Historic Environment, of the National Planning Policy Framework (NPPF) and (for Wales) in Welsh Office Circular 61/96 - Planning and the Historic Environment: Historic Buildings and Conservation Areas.

There are additional planning controls over certain works carried out within the conservation area. For example, demolition within conservation areas requires consent. Trees are another very sensitive subject.

The designation does not preclude development from taking place, but does require that developments preserve or enhance the historic character of the area, for example, by ensuring that newly constructed buildings are of a high-quality design. Conservation area status also removes some permitted development rights that apply in undesignated areas.

## Designation of Conservation Areas

Local authorities are chiefly responsible for designating conservation areas. They can designate any area of 'special architectural or historic interest' whose character or appearance is worth protecting or enhancing. Local and regional criteria are used, rather than any national standard. In exceptional circumstances, English Heritage can designate conservation areas in London, but it has to consult the relevant Borough Council and obtain the consent of the Secretary of State for Culture Media and Sport. The Secretary of State can also designate in exceptional circumstances – usually where the area is of more than local interest.

Local authorities have additional powers under planning legislation to control changes to buildings in a conservation area, which might usually be allowed without planning permission in other locations, for example, changing the appearance of windows, adding external cladding, or putting up satellite dishes.

## Design of New Development

A very high standard of design sympathetic to the existing environment is required when submitting a planning application within a conservation area. New development must make a positive contribution to the character of the area. In view of this, your council can require additional information in support of any planning application, showing how the proposal will relate to the conservation area. This can mean the submission of elevations of neighbouring buildings, full details of the proposal, and examples of materials and colours.

## Apply to carry out building work on a property in a conservation area.

Many cities, towns, and villages contain areas of architectural or historic interest. A number of these have been designated as conservation areas.
The ultimate success of conservation areas will depend upon the care that individual owners take in the maintenance and repair of their properties and in any alterations or extensions they make. Your local area planning office can provide you with advice and guidance on development in conservation areas. Therefore, any application to carry out works would need to show significant desire to maintain and improve the relationship between the building and its conservation.

### Permitted Development in Conservation Areas

Permitted development (PD) rights still exist in conservation areas but are curtailed in some instances (probably not by as much as you might think). Here is a summary of the key rules.

**Extensions:** In a conservation area, you will need to apply for planning permission for any extension other than a single storey rear extension of no more than 3 m (or 4 m if the house is detached).

Side extensions and two-storey extensions – some of which are permissible under PD rights in other areas – are all excluded from PD rights in a conservation area.

**Recladding:** If you live in a conservation area, you will need to apply for planning permission before cladding the outside of your house with stone, artificial stone, pebbledash, render, timber, plastic, or tiles.

**Windows:** This is a bit of a grey area, but unless your conservation area home is subject to an Article 4 direction removing permitted development rights, you can, in theory, replace your existing windows with new windows and doors that are of a similar appearance to those used in the construction of the house.

Simply put, the rules in a conservation area are the same as those in a regular non-designated area, so you will still need permission for a radically different window scheme (including new openings).

**Outbuildings:** Conservation area homeowners have the same PD rights as regular homeowners, with the exception of the ability to erect an outbuilding to the side of the house. Other regular PD rights prohibit outbuildings to the front of the property, place height restrictions particularly near boundaries, and state that they shouldn't cover more than half of the area of land around the house.

**Solar panels:** This is a controversial area recently for obvious reasons, but in theory, if you're in a conservation area, you won't need planning approval for a solar panel unless the solar panel is wall-mounted (not on your roof) on a wall facing the highway. So, if you've got a south-facing house in a conservation area, you can install panels on your roof, provided certain limitations are met.

### Enforcement

In practice, enforcement of conservation areas varies – depending on the resources and priorities of the local authority – and many fail to meet expectations. A conservation area may have a conservation area advisory committee: a non-elected body of people, some of whom may be expert, who are concerned about the conservation in the particular area. Historic England maintains an 'at risk' register, which includes conservation areas.

# 11

# Structural Engineers

You may not realise, but most builds involve some form of structural design, usually to be integrated within the Building Regulations process. This can be anything from foundations design in case of unstable ground to incorporating steel beams within the build. Often, the architect would initiate this, as the engineer's design is incorporated in the drawings. But, subject to the build and the architect's brief, you may find yourself employing the engineer for this work.

Before work can begin, structural engineers are often involved in the investigation and survey of the site to determine the suitability of the earth for the requirements of the upcoming project.

If you plan to build with Timber Frame, since there is a great deal of timber engineering, any structural calculations would be included in their package. However, if there are ground considerations requiring design, you would more than likely still require a separate structural engineer as the timber frame co would only design their own element above DPC.

Even if your works are modest in size, once the necessity for a structural engineer arises, then the works automatically require Building Regulations approval.

Structural engineering forms the basis of all buildings, therefore we could say that has been around since humans first started constructing their own structures. It became a more defined and formalised profession with the emergence of the architecture profession, as distinct from the engineering profession, during the industrial revolution in the late nineteenth century. Until then, the architect and the structural engineer were usually one - the master builder. Only with the development of specialised knowledge of structural theories that emerged during the nineteenth and early twentieth centuries did the professional structural engineer come into existence.

The structural engineer is interested in the strength and stability of the elements of construction - the solid sections between the architect's 'spaces', like the floor or wall between rooms, and would also be concerned with the safety, efficiency, and elegance of buildings and engineering structures. They work with other professionals in design and construction, but take particular responsibility for how buildings and other structures respond to loadings considering the weight of the building itself, the contents - including people - and how the building reacts with the ground. Designs must not only be sufficiently safe but also efficient and easy to build.

Many structural engineers work in design, whilst some are in involved in contracting and actually building the structures. When it comes to individual homes, however, it is quite unusual to employ a structural engineer to design a house from scratch; it is more common for them to be asked to work on an existing idea or design possibly in conjunction with another design professional.

The role of the structural engineer is a key component in the construction process. Part of the wider discipline of civil engineering, structural engineering is concerned with the design and physical integrity of buildings and other large structures. Structural engineers have a wide range of responsibilities - not least a duty to ensure the safety and durability of the project on which they are working.

Unlike architects, who must focus on the appearance, shape, size, and use of the building, structural engineers must solve technical problems and help the architect achieve his or her vision for the project.

Structural engineers have to choose appropriate materials, such as concrete, steel, timber, and masonry to meet design specifications. When construction has begun, they are often involved in inspecting the work and advising contractors.

They also examine existing buildings and structures to test if they are structurally sound and still fit for purpose. Although the structural engineer's job does not include physically building the structure, it is imperative that they understand construction processes. A good engineer will ensure 'constructability'; that the structure will not be unnecessarily difficult to build and will be built properly.

Tasks may vary depending on the structure being worked on and size of the team, but can include:

- Analysing configurations of the basic structural components of a building or other structure.
- Calculating the pressures, stresses, and strains that each component, such as a beam or lintel, will experience

from other parts of the structure due to human use or environmental pressures such as weather.

- Considering the strength of various materials, for example, timber, concrete, steel, and brick, to see how their inclusion may necessitate a change of structural design.
- Liaising with other designers, including architects and project managers, to agree on safe designs and their fit with the aesthetic concept of the construction.
- Examining structures at risk of collapse and advising how to improve their structural integrity, such as recommending removal or repair of defective parts or rebuilding the entire structure.
- Making drawings, specifications, and computer models of structures for building contractors.
- Working with geotechnical engineers to investigate ground conditions and analyse results of soil sample and in situ tests;
- Liaising with construction contractors to ensure that newly erected buildings are structurally sound.
- Applying expert knowledge of the forces that act on various structures.
- Using computers and computer-aided design (CAD) technology for simulation purposes.

## Qualifications of a Structural Engineer

Before you try to find a structural engineer, it is worth knowing what to look for in one. All structural engineers, including a trainee structural engineer, should have some sort of structural engineering qualifications.

A degree, usually in civil or structural engineering, must be obtained first. This is followed by a training period that can last up to 4 years. Whilst this may seem like overkill, structural engineering is a very serious job with potentially fatal consequences if the job is done wrong, so a thorough understanding is crucial. Be sure to check with any potential engineers about the structural engineer courses they have undertaken.

Because of the safety issues involved in their work, structural engineers must be trained to strict standards. Most structural engineering courses require a related undergraduate degree in an engineering discipline. After graduation, structural engineers work towards professional qualifications - becoming Associated and then Chartered Members with the Institution of Structural Engineers.

Depending on the degree course they have studied and / or the jurisdiction they are seeking licensure in, they may be accredited (or licensed) as just structural engineers, or as civil engineers, or as both civil and structural engineers.

## Finding the Right Engineer

A good place to start your search is The Institution of Structural Engineers, the world's leading professional body for qualifications and standards in structural engineering. To become a member, engineers have to go through a rigorous entry programme, including a thorough interview and examinations that test for professional competence. The institution has 27,000 members in over 100 countries, so you're sure to find a local accredited structural engineer near you!

When you have found a few local structural engineers, ask to see their qualifications, public liability insurance, and a list of references and / or portfolio. You should also ask for a quote, as this will allow you to compare costs and work out a fair price.

Once you have found a suitable structural engineer and agreed on a quote, you should draw up a contract signed by both sides. This allows both sides to have realistic expectations, as well as something to fall back upon if anything were to not go according to contract.

### How Much Does it Cost?

The costs involved will ultimately depend on the scale and complexity involved in the project.

You will find that most structural engineers will quote per hour, and you can expect to pay anywhere between £50 - £150.

# 12

# Energy Performance Calculations

We now explore the energy performance model which includes, and is included in, numerous aspects of the design:

SAP (Standard Assessment Procedure) is a requirement of the Building Regulations, and is essential for all newly built dwellings in the UK.

This process has been adopted by government as part of the UK national standard to calculate the energy performance of buildings, and it is used to assess and compare the energy and environmental performance of dwellings. Its purpose is to provide accurate and reliable assessments of dwelling energy performances that are needed to underpin energy and environmental policy initiatives.

SAP is usually conducted in two stages: dwelling emission rate (DER) and target emission rate (TER) are created as the design values, which are then re-modelled as an 'as-built' calculation when the eventual works (including an air leakage test) are completed. This is a very complex calculation and requires a specialist.

A SAP rating has been required for all new homes under Part L of the Building Regulations since 1995; therefore, most developers will be familiar with it.

Every new house has to have a SAP rating. It provides a simple means of reliably estimating the energy efficiency performance of your home. However, for many first time self-builders and developers, it will be a new and often challenging aspect of the planning and building control process.

You may also need a SAP for a conversion or extension - but slightly different rules apply. SAPs for Scotland also have different requirements.

SAP ratings are expressed on a scale of 1 to 100 - the higher the number, the better the rating. Thus, it is similar to the fuel consumption of a car under standard driving conditions. SAP is calculated by a procedure specified in Building Regulations, and which predicts heating and hot water costs.

These costs depend on the insulation and air tightness of the house, and on the efficiency and control of the heating system. The calculation uses the Building Research Establishment's Domestic Energy Model (BREDEM).

In order to meet current Building Regulations, home builders will need to gain a 'pass' on their SAP calculations. Without it, Building Control will not sign off the development, and the property cannot be let or marketed for sale.

But there are other reasons to care about SAP.

A SAP assessor can help the designer or architect to shape the energy profile of a new dwelling – minimise its energy use and carbon emissions.

The effect of different construction types, heating systems, and technologies can be accurately measured and, in turn, incorporated within the build.

Another key point is that the SAP rating indicates the energy performance of the property, and in turn provides the Energy Performance Certificate (EPC) that all buyers and tenants consider.

A 'pass' is gained by meeting several compliance targets around:

- How well the fabric of the dwelling contains heat
- Solar gain
- Quality of construction and commissioning of systems
- Predicted $CO_2$ emissions from the dwelling

SAP works by assessing how much energy a dwelling will consume when delivering a defined level of comfort and service provision. The assessment is based on standardised assumptions for occupancy and behaviour. This enables a like-for-like comparison of dwelling performance. Related factors, such as fuel costs and emissions of carbon dioxide ($CO_2$), can be determined from the assessment.

SAP quantifies a dwelling's performance in terms of energy use per unit floor area, a fuel-cost-based energy efficiency rating (the SAP rating), and emissions of $CO_2$ (the environmental impact rating).

These indicators of performance are based on estimates of annual energy consumption for the provision of space heating, domestic hot water, lighting, and ventilation. Other SAP outputs include estimate of appliance energy use, the potential for overheating in summer, and the resultant cooling load.

The headline emissions target is achieved using the DER / TER figures. $CO_2$ emissions are measured by comparing the TER against the predicted DER. This target rate is set within SAP by reference to a notional dwelling of the same size and shape, using a set of baseline values.

More importantly, these $CO_2$ figures are now increasingly used by planners and councils to drive other objectives – from meeting sustainability targets and local renewable energy policy to determining 106-type community contributions.

### Fabric Energy Efficiency

Homes built after April 2014 in England are also assessed on fabric energy efficiency. This is not a measure of carbon but energy demand in units of kilowatt-hours per square metre per year. How well a home retains the heat it produces will have an impact on its $CO_2$ emissions as well as on its separate assessment to gauge compliance.

Fabric energy efficiency is assessed using Design and Target figures. As with emissions, the target is set within SAP using a set of baseline values depending on the size of the property.

### What's Involved in the process?

A SAP assessor will work from architect's plans and construction detail, together with a full heating, ventilation, and air conditioning (HVAC) specification. For this reason drawings must be scaled accurately and must show all elevations, sections, and floor and site plans.

The assessor will scale off of these plans either electronically or by hand to create a model of the dwelling(s) in SAP software.

Once the site form is established, the heating, lighting, and ventilation systems are added - specific products are picked from manufacturer databases where they are known.

All thermal elements (walls, floors, roofs, and openings) are added in detail together with all calculations for thermal junctions. Any renewable technologies and cooling are also added.

Once complete, a SAP calculation is capable of producing a raft of detailed reporting outputs, from site form, heat losses, and energy demand to seasonal variations, $CO_2$ emissions and renewables contributions, to name just a few.

## How Do I Ensure a Pass?

It's fair to say that developers and architects didn't pay much attention to SAP in the old days - but since the significant changes in 2005, SAP 2009, and again in 2014, complying with the SAP regulations and in turn Part L of Building Regulations has become a whole lot tougher.

This is primarily because $CO_2$ emissions targets have tightened enormously - driven as they are by European and UK climate policies. An average new build designed just 5 years ago is unlikely to pass SAP regs today.

It is incredibly important to understand that many factors contribute to a SAP rating. Assessors are often asked to explain why some builds fail and some pass, and it isn't always easy to give a straight answer. Numerous factors can play a part: from the size of a boiler to a junction in a wall, to the thickness of insulation in a floor, to which direction the house is pointing!

Some factors may be beyond your control – for example, having no connection to mains gas could mean having to use an oil or LPG system. These fuels have higher cost and $CO_2$ emissions factors within SAP, and as the target emission rate is set based on a mains gas system, you are likely to take a hit.

If we ignore the wider climate change issues, resist technicalities, and assume we are not trying to produce a zero carbon house, we can tie down a few good principles which will give you a good chance of success:

**1. Minimum U-values are there to be beaten, not followed.**
If the fabric of the building is well insulated, you may not need renewable technologies to get you through. Design as much insulation into the walls, floors, and roofs as you possibly can.

**2. Windows and doors lose a lot of heat.**
Pay attention to the U-values on the openings you are specifying and get them as low as possible.

**3. It's not the boiler, it's the controls.**
Zoned heating and load/weather compensators for boilers will often have a more significant effect on the SAP rating than the system itself.

**4. Airtightness.**
All new builds require air permeability testing on completion, and the resulting figure goes into the SAP calculations. Make sure the envelope is sealed and even get a pre-test check carried out.

**5. Thermal bridging.**
Thermal bridging refers to heat loss through junctions with external walls. Follow a scheme such as Accredited Construction Details (ACDs) or Enhanced Construction Details (ECDs).

**Start Early!**

The one key point - even more important than those above - is to **start early.**

To address the subject of SAP halfway through a build means that there's not a lot that can be done to change the energy performance of that building. This scenario also leads to much bad practice and usually, the installation of unsuitable, expensive technologies added in hindsight just to pass Building Regulations or to meet a planning condition.

Avoid this by engaging with your SAP assessor as early in the process as possible - often this will be well before planning has even been submitted, and certainly well before Building Regulations applications.

# 13

# Code for Sustainable Homes

Although technically, the government withdrew the Code for Sustainable Homes (CSH) earlier this year (2015), there are still many planning approvals or part-finished projects that still fall under the scheme. Under certain circumstances, the condition stipulating CSH inclusion can be appealed or a request can be made to have it withdrawn in lieu of other sustainability measures that form part of the local authorities' planning policies.

Elements of the CSH are now incorporated into Building Regulations, and will be retitled as the 'new national technical standards' and set at the equivalent of a Code Level 4. Building Research Establishment (BRE) has said it will continue to certify schemes under the code, and the body have launched a new national quality mark for consumers to help them understand the changes.

However, for the sake of this chapter, I will carry on to explain the CSH as there are many aspects that are still relevant.

The Code for Sustainable Homes is / was an environmental assessment method for rating and certifying the performance of new homes based on BRE Global's EcoHomes and to create a national standard intended to encourage continuous improvement in sustainable home building.

## Scope and Scoring

The Code works by awarding new homes a rating effectively from Level 3 to Level 6, based on their performance against nine sustainability criteria, which are combined to assess the overall environmental impact. Level 3 is considered entry level above Building Regulations, and Level 6 is the highest, reflecting exemplary developments in terms of sustainability. Level 4 is now considered the standard to be reached within Building Regulations.

Many assume that you need expensive renewables and technologies to achieve Code Level 4. In fact, by taking a 'fabric-first' approach – ensuring the performance of the building envelope is to a high level – these expenses can be avoided. However, it is very important to consider this early in the design phase.

The sustainability criteria by which new homes are measured are:

- **Energy and $CO_2$ emissions** – Operational Energy and resulting emissions of carbon dioxide to the atmosphere (different minimum standards that must be met at each level of the Code).

- **Water** – Internal and external water saving measures specified (minimum standards that must be met at each level of the Code).
- **Materials** – Sourcing and environmental impact of materials used to build the home (minimum standards present).
- **Surface water run-off** – Management of surface water run-off from the development and flood risk (minimum standards present).
- **Waste** – Storage for recyclable waste and compost, and care taken to reduce, reuse, and recycle construction materials (minimum standards present).
- **Pollution** –Use of insulation materials and heating systems that do not add to global warming.
- **Health and well-being** – Provision of good daylight quality, sound insulation, private space, accessibility, and adaptability (minimum standards present for Code Level 6 only).
- **Management** – A Home User Guide, designing in security, and reducing the impact of construction.
- **Ecology** – Protection and enhancement of the ecology of the area and efficient use of building land.

There are mandatory performance requirements in six categories. All other performance requirements are flexible. It is possible to achieve an overall level depending on the mandatory standards and proportion of flexible standards achieved.

## Compliance

Once it is established that a Code for Sustainable Homes is required, it is important that an accredited CSH assessor is appointed at an early stage.

Often, pre-assessments are required by local planning authorities to demonstrate that the development has the capability of meeting a CSH standard. The requirement to meet this standard is then incorporated in a binding planning condition.

Prior to starting the development, it is best practice to engage the CSH assessor to undertake and have certificated a 'Design Stage' assessment.

The assessor should work closely with you and your architect to agree which credits are to be targeted in which areas. In order to achieve design stage certification, you will have to commit to meeting these targets, and your architect should incorporate the measures into the design specification.

You will probably have to commission additional reports, such as an ecological report or flood risk assessments.

Upon completion of the development, the CSH assessor will undertake a post-construction review to establish that the credits targeted and the measures specified have been undertaken. The assessor will then complete their report and submit this to the accreditation body to facilitate final certification.

# 14

# Schedule of Works

**The schedule of works (SoW) is the Bible of Construction Project Management!**

In order to receive accurate quotations from contractors, a document literally spelling out the works involved, as a list, should be created. I cannot emphasise enough how valuable a schedule of works is in whatever form. It should also incorporate certain specifications and details that will ensure like-for-like quotations. You cannot have too much information in a SoW since just the architect's detail drawings are not enough for contractors to provide accurate quotations. The document should be looked upon as the kingpin of the whole build procedure.

Some may call it a scope of works, but scope or schedule, the object of the exercise is to create a document that gives clear, accurate lists of the works to be executed. The document is in effect a directory of the works to be agreed upon between the client and the contractor; so it should have as much information regarding each item as possible to avoid any ambiguity at either the tendering stage or during work execution.

In short, it becomes the Works Bible!

A schedule of works outlines the specific tasks that need to be completed in the construction process, but it can become quite complex as it must cross-refer to its supporting documents.

The SoW, exactly as issued for tendering purposes, is also used on site by the contractor's workforce on a day-to-day basis to determine the work to be executed during construction. For use on site, the SoW and accompanying documents must not only identify the materials and allow calculation of quantities involved, but they must also give precise instructions on where all the materials are to be used and how they are to be incorporated together. It should also set out an ordered arrangement of tasks to be carried out in the correct sequence to achieve the desired end result.

One aspect of the SoW that should not be in dispute is its general form and purpose, and for this book, the essence of a SoW could hardly be simpler. It is a list – in this case a list, either in outline or detail, of building work. In common with any list, it may be used for different purposes, by different people at different times, and may be accompanied by, or bound with, other documents.

Schedules of works are 'without quantities' instructional lists produced in smaller projects for alteration work or new builds. They are alternatives to bills of quantities, allowing pricing of items, such as builders' work, and fixing schedules (such as sanitary fittings, doors, windows, ironmongery, and light fittings).

Schedules of works are prepared by designers rather than the cost consultant. They may be prepared as part of the production information alongside drawings, specifications, bills of quantities, and preliminaries and should form part of the tender documentation, and then any contract documents.

A schedule is a description of the work required to be executed. Any information about quality should be provided by reference to specifications, and information about location and size should be provided on drawings.

Schedules should allow the contractor to identify significant work and materials that will be needed to complete the works and to calculate the quantities that will be required at a particular time. As a consequence, it is important that schedules of works thoroughly describe every significant item of work to which they relate. Failure to do so may result in a claim by the contractor for additional works 'not allowed for'.

Schedules of works can be arranged on an elemental basis (for example, groundwork, concrete, masonry, and so on) or on a room-by-room basis.

Even simple building work can require detailed description, and the schedule of work is usually accompanied by other documents providing information supplementing the listed items, including:

- **Drawings** - To illustrate extent of the work;
- **Schedules** - Itemised lists of particular product types, commonly doors, windows, ironmongery, finishes, and decorations;
- **Some form of specification** - To describe the standards to which each category of work is to be carried out; and
- **Preliminaries** - To determine general requirements for the project as a whole, often with reference to a particular standard form of building contract.

**Differing Uses Throughout a Project:**

A simple list can serve a number of uses, and the SoW is no different. Together with the supporting documents, it may be used in the following ways as a:

- Tender document
- Contract document
- Task list for work on site
- Checklist for administration
- Record document

**As part of the tender document:**

The purpose of the SoW at tendering stage is to provide sufficient description of the proposals to allow a number of independent building contractors (usually a minimum of three) to calculate fair and, hopefully, competitive prices for the work. In general, this task will be undertaken by quantity surveyors (who may be employed directly by the contractor, and are then generally referred to as 'estimators'). They will price listed items to determine the overall cost.
The descriptions in the SoW must be unambiguous. They need not be complete in themselves, but may cross-refer to the accompanying documents - particularly to the drawings. However, they must cover, at least in outline, all aspects of the work for which prices are required. Together, the information provided must allow the contractor to identify all the materials needed and to calculate the quantities that will be required.

The original SoW and supporting documents, together with descriptions of variations from the work originally intended, may be archived as an 'as-built' document within the health and safety file, set for record purposes. In certain instances, if serious faults are found later, the SoW, as part of this document set, will again be studied in detail.

In general, it is essential that the SoW be read, and understood, by perhaps four or more sets of people – Designer, Engineer, Contractor, Q.S, who must each be able to use the document (and its supporting documents) to gain a particular understanding of the building. The extent to which these aims may be met depends largely on the structure of the schedule of works itself. There must be a methodology behind the description that relates closely to the type and extent of the work being carried out.

Having said all of the above, a schedule of works does not need to be an overly elaborate document and should be formed in perspective with the job. Above, I refer to a SoW that would perhaps incorporate certain quantities and specifications. It could be argued that a straightforward extension does not require quite as much of a schedule as a new build of 5,000 sq. ft. However, all projects should have a SoW of some form.

Another purpose of the document is to furthermore provide information regarding e.g. – you (the client), the site itself, a brief description of the works, drawing numbers, any existing ground considerations, demolition work, site rules, payment agreements. These are the preambles that help to paint the picture of the job and allow any contractor to include the less obvious items (for example, no mains electricity yet so a generator may be needed).

In theory, Mr & Mrs Self-Build **can** create the schedule of works themselves, but only if they have serious construction knowledge. It is imperative that the SoW provide precise information, especially on below-ground items, where the potential contractor's knowledge is only as good as the information that you give him.

Let me give you an example page of a SoW created for a recent job that had two sewers running across the site. The new build was shoehorned between the two:

2.2.1.1 **Note: There are two existing foul sewers running across the site. One (FS1) to the immediate right of the proposed, as shown on drawing 103, which is a 150 mm dia at approx. 2.4 m depth. The second (FS2), as shown in Appendix 1, Drainage search, is what appears to be a 300 mm dia pipe at a similar depth. Allowances must be made for any shuttering / shoring of trenches to achieve foundation depths as indicated in Pattern drawing SK01 in Appendix B adjacent to FS2. Assume necessary permission to build over or near a sewer is granted from Thames Water, organised by client.**

2.2.1.2 Foundation adjacent to FS1 to be taken down to invert level (assume 2.4 m) and stepped according to 2.3.1.4.

2.2.1.3 Excavate foundation trenches to the widths indicated on the drawings. Allow for an overall foundation depth of min 1 m (see note 2.3.1.2) other than where indicated. Bottom of trench to be level and compacted. Steps in foundations must not be of a greater dimension than the thickness of the foundation. Where foundations are stepped (on elevation), they should overlap by twice the height of the step, and step in height by no more than the dimension width of the foundation, or 300 mm - whichever is the greater. No steps to be closer than 600 mm from any corner.

**2.2.1.4 Install below ground steelwork as shown in pattern drawing SL01 in Appendix B.**

**2.2.1.5 Set aside spoil for backfill; cart way all remaining spoil.**

**2.2.1.6 Pour concrete foundation consisting of ready mix concrete FDN 2 or similar to the levels shown in the drawings. Trowel to a level finish.**

Accompanied by the drawings, the preceding information would provide sufficient details to accurately quantify and, therefore, quote for the works. The appendices would show the structural engineer's design, a soil report, and the water board search (which would show the positions, depths, and sizes of the sewers).

With these details, you are telling the contractor, first, that the sewers exist; second, where they are located and the ground conditions; and third, what he should quote for. Sometimes, with unknown quantities, a request for a unit rate should be included so any additional works (for example, 'The sewer was deeper so we had more muck-away') can be agreed in principle beforehand.

One other consideration is that, in the case of the above sample, with such specific information, it is entirely possible that some contractors could feel out of their depth (literally) so would decline to quote. This is good; the last thing you want is having the wrong contractor (you want the right person in the right place) commence works only to find out that the works are more involved than his experience.

Now, it is entirely possible that the data that you have provided has an inaccuracy (the position as specified by the water board as to the sewer's position and depth), but you have provided as much information as possible. But equally important is that all quotes received should then be like for like. In this instance, a contingency amount would be allowed, just in case that the water board information is incorrect.

From a project management perspective, yes, you would quite likely employ a quantity surveyor to create the SoW, but it is your job to collate all the relevant information to give to him – in this example, the water board search, the soil report, and the structural engineer's design. A quantity surveyor also is only as good as the information at his fingertips.

Clearly, not all projects involve an aspect requiring such a deep (excuse the pun) and meaningful explanation and instruction; but my point is, the more information you provide, the more accurate the quotation, and the more likelihood that the eventual chosen contractor can initate the works smoothly.

The SoW document should be priced at each independent item, making it clear as to how the job is estimated. When sending out to individual element contractors (groundworks, brickworks, carpentry, and so on), it is then easy for you to state and itemise exactly which items each contractor should quote to ensure that all items are covered. None of this 'I thought that the plumber had included that' sort of conversation should occur later. I always send out the entire document to every contractor, just informing them which items to quote for. This provides the bigger picture and encourages the contractor to perhaps include (or not) other items which he may consider part of his brief.

A note – 'or any other items not covered' is a useful inclusion to the page to guarantee all bases are covered.

When pricing a good SoW, the contractor will put figures against each item, which makes it very easy when working out what should or should not be paid for at each payment stage. Likewise, if an item is omitted, the amount to be deducted becomes apparent.

In reality, the schedules of works that I create are possibly seen as too elaborate, and you must take your own view. However, I have been that building contractor who, since he was not given sufficient information, either priced too safe, making his quote too dear, or did not include for enough of the eventual works and became caught up in the argument, 'I thought that was included in your quotation'. With that in mind, I try very hard on behalf of my clients to ensure that by the time we shake hands with each contractor, we have a very clear view of what the works will involve and how much they will cost.

# 15

# Surveys

Surveys are an effective way of gathering information to be used at numerous stages of the proceedings.

There are numerous survey requirements that you could come across, and although the majority of what we will explore in this chapter usually relates to a new build, some requirements still apply to a conversion / refurb.

## Topographical Survey

Topographical surveys are used to identify and map the contours of the ground and existing features on the surface of the site, or slightly above or below the Earth's surface (for example, trees, buildings, roads, manholes, utility poles, retaining walls, and so on).

The purpose of the survey is to serve as a base map for the design of a building, road, or driveway; it would usually include the showing of perimeter boundary lines.

Topographical surveys relate to local ordinance survey 'benchmarks' from which all ground contours are mapped. Therefore, information regarding surface and underground utilities, sewers, and so on are all determined by these levels. Benchmarks are taken from mean sea level; so the increase in the number shown on the map is representative of the increase upwards from sea level and is, therefore, higher.

This type of survey is an accurate representation of the area showing all natural and manmade features with levels. Shown as level reference points, all elements including the property, land features, and physical boundary details are presented on a scaled survey drawing. The amount of detail included in a topographical survey depends on your requirements; but typically, the land survey will include existing buildings and structures, boundary details, a grid of levels, ground surfaces, tree positions, drainage details, and service chamber cover positions. Additional details can be included, such as the features adjacent to the site or underground services. Survey drawings are normally delivered as CAD files and as scaled paper plans.

A topo survey is useful to the architect and certain trades, such as ground workers, to show and determine the actual site levels in relation to any proposed levels.

The survey includes the indication of a base level or datum that all other marked levels relate to. This would be a static position, which will not be altered or moved during the course of the works, such as a manhole cover in the road.

Quite often, the provision of a topo survey drawing would be a planning condition.

## Site Investigation / Soil Survey

Soil survey, or soil mapping, is the process of classifying soil types and other soil properties in a given area and geo-encoding such information. It applies the principles of soil science and draws heavily from geomorphology theories of soil formation, physical geography, and analysis of vegetation and land use patterns. Primary data for the soil survey are acquired by field sampling and remote sensing.

The correct terminology for this type of survey is geotechnical or geoenvironmental, and the object of the exercise is primarily to confirm the suitability of ground conditions for below ground works - whether it is piled foundations, retaining walls, slope stability, or any project where a full understanding of the soil and rock characteristics is required.

There are fundamentally two types of surveys - a desktop study and intrusive investigation. Both should be carried out according to UK CLR11 guidelines.

**Desktop study**
A Phase I investigation or desk study is the collation and review of published information about a site. The Phase I investigation is normally carried out at the start of the site investigation process to characterise the site and inform the remainder of the site investigation. In addition to reviewing the published information, a detailed inspection of the site (walkover survey) is normally undertaken. It is an integral part of the phased approach to site investigation.

The benefits of carrying out a Phase I investigation prior to commencing intrusive works include:

- Efficient targeting of project resource allocation.
- Formulation of the preliminary geological ground model.
- Early identification of potential geohazards.
- Prevention of money wastage on inappropriate intrusive ground investigations.
- Early warning of possible delays or budget implications through previously unknown site characteristics.
- Information on possible contaminants and anticipated areas of contamination.

Desk studies draw upon historical ordnance survey maps, aerial photography, Environment Agency databases, British Geological Survey records, and many other sources.

**Intrusive survey**

A Phase II intrusive investigation comprises obtaining samples and carrying out testing from exploratory holes to obtain information about the ground conditions. The exploratory holes may include hand- or machine-excavated trial pits, mini rig boring, light cable percussive boring, or rotary boring, depending on the findings of the Phase I investigation and the requirements of the investigation.

The exploratory holes enable a programme of in-situ testing, laboratory testing, and monitoring to be undertaken, culminating in a report that includes a revised risk assessment and conceptual ground model.

## Ground Gas Survey

### Radon

The radioactive gas Radon is a hazard in many homes and workplaces. Breathing in radon is the second largest cause of lung cancer in the UK resulting in up to 2000 fatal cancers per year. Naturally occurring, it is particularly prevalent in granite and limestone areas but not exclusively so. Radon levels vary not only between different parts of the country but even between neighbouring buildings.

The principal areas of the country in which radon is a problem are the granite areas of Cornwall and Devon, and the limestone areas of Derbyshire, Northamptonshire, North Oxfordshire, Lincolnshire, and Somerset, however there are many other areas in England and Wales affected by radon.

Concentrations in the open air are very low. However radon that enters enclosed spaces, such as buildings, can reach relatively high concentrations in some circumstances. Radon from the ground is drawn into buildings through cracks and gaps because the atmospheric pressure inside the building can be slightly lower than the pressure in the underlying soil.

Radon is a naturally occurring radioactive gas, which is produced by the radioactive decay of radium which, in turn, is derived from the radioactive decay of uranium.

Uranium is found in small quantities in all soils and rocks, although the amount varies from place to place. Radon released from rocks and soils is quickly diluted in the atmosphere. Concentrations in the open air are normally very low and do not present a hazard.

Radon that enters buildings may reach high concentrations in some circumstances. The construction method and degree of ventilation will influence radon levels in individual buildings. A person's exposure to radon will also vary according to how particular buildings and spaces are used.

Radon and other ground gases, such as Methane, are now more recognised as contributors to health and safety in buildings and in commonly known effected areas, precautions now form part of a Building Regulation or Planning condition. A desk based on-line search can be done to locate the risk of radon at your property.

The outcome of any radon search will categorise the ground around the property in 3 ways

- No action required
- A basic radon barrier system installation required
- A full positive ventilation radon control system installation required

The latter two require the introduction of additional materials and installation techniques to create a system to provide the level of protection designated.

## Landfill Gas

Landfill gas occurs when the organic content of household waste is broken down by bacteria into Methane ($CH_4$) and Carbon dioxide ($CO_2$). The production of landfill gas is a recent problem as the organic waste content of landfills has increased since the introduction of the first Clean Air Act in 1956. Before this, most domestic waste was burnt and so landfill sites contained a high proportion of ash, a material that does not generate large quantities of landfill gas. It should also be noted that it is not just domestic waste landfills that produce gases, industrial and demolition waste landfills may also have the potential to generate large quantities of landfill gas.

Both Methane and Carbon dioxide are odourless and colourless and it is only the presence of trace gases that produces the distinctive landfill gas odour. There are many hundreds of types of trace gases but most do not usually represent a health hazard following normal atmospheric dilution.

## Ground Gas

Ground gas is mainly composed of Methane and Carbon dioxide and presents similar risks to that of landfill gas. Ground gas can be formed by natural or man-made means. The following are common sources and their typical components:

- Peat bogs and mosslands ($CH_4$, $CO_2$)
- Uranium bearing rocks such as granites (Radon)
- Carbonate rocks such as limestone and chalk ($CO_2$)
- Organic rich rocks such as coal measures ($CH_4$, $CO_2$, $H_2S$)
- River and lake sediments ($CH_4$, $CO_2$, $H_2S$)
- Made ground (ground that has been formed by the activities of man and can consist of natural or man made materials) ($CH_4$, $CO_2$, $H_2S$, VOCs and any other gas)
- Farmland
- Sewers

Precautions need to be taken for Methane as it may give rise to a variety of hazards if it migrates to, and accumulates in, a property or confined spaces. If generated in sufficient quantity the gas may form an explosive mixture with air. It can also act as an asphyxiant and in particular circumstances it may be toxic.

Carbon dioxide is an asphyxiating gas and causes adverse health effects, unconsciousness or even death at relatively low concentrations (at approximately 5% by volume in air).

The primary way that testing is carried out is that holes are drilled into the ground, pipes inserted, monitoring equipment installed and the information from the equipment is recorded over a period of months. The depth, amount of holes and frequency of monitoring is dependent on the site and its previous uses, for instance an untouched green field site is less likely to be subjected to intensive testing compared to a former petro chemical factory site that is adjacent to a landfill site!

How do you protect a structure against ground gases?

The measures required to protect a building against the effects of ground gases can be very complex, which is why there is so much legislation about the subject. A brief overview is as follows.

First of all it starts with analysing all the data from your testing and bore holes, once you have collated all this information you carry out a risk assessment.

This determines the risk or likelihood of ground gases getting into a structure and that will determine what needs to be done to give the best protection to that building and these might include.

- Changes to the way the building is going to be built
- Additional landscaping around the building
- Positive or negative pressure ventilation systems
- Installation of ground gas membranes

The installation of a ground gas membrane to a structure is one the easiest ways to make the property more resistant to ground gases.

## Asbestos Survey

An asbestos survey would only usually be required if demolishing or tearing apart an existing building, and is a health & safety requirement incorporated within the CDM (Construction Design Management) documents.

Asbestos remains one of the most problematic health hazards in domestic, commercial, industrial, and public buildings today. If asbestos based material is found in good condition and undisturbed, it presents no risks. However, we all need to take extreme care to comply with changing legislation when carrying out building reviews, remediation, or demolition.

Furthermore, if you have property that was constructed pre-2000 and plan to undertake refurbishment or demolition work, then you require a refurbishment and demolition survey. These are legislative requirements as laid down and monitored by the Health and Safety Executive (HSE) and would form part of your recently revised CDM requirements, as discussed in a different chapter.

Surveys vary significantly in terms of size and complexity. Both access and visibility can be simple or complex. Moreover, the presence of asbestos can vary depending on the age, structure, and design of the property.

Fundamentally, there are two different surveys that relate to the domestic environment.

**Management surveys (Formerly type 2 asbestos surveys)**
This is the core survey to locate, as far as reasonably practicable, the presence and extent of any suspected Asbestos Containing Materials (ACMs), in order to assess their condition and to provide a risk assessment on any disturbance. This is a minimally intrusive survey, but it is not usually relevant to domestic construction works.

**Refurbishment and demolition surveys (Formerly type 3 asbestos surveys)**
A refurbishment and demolition survey is needed before any refurbishment or demolition work is carried out. This type of survey is used to locate and describe, as far as reasonably practicable, all ACMs in the area where the refurbishment work will take place, or in the whole building if demolition is planned. The survey is fully intrusive and involves destructive inspection, as necessary, to gain access to all areas, including those that may be difficult to reach.

There is a specific requirement in CAR 2012 (Regulation 7) for all ACMs to be removed as far as reasonably practicable before major refurbishment or final demolition. Removing ACMs is also appropriate in other smaller refurbishment situations that involve structural or layout changes to buildings (for example, removal of partitions, walls, units, and so on). Under CDM, the survey information should be used to help in the tendering process before work starts. The survey report should be supplied by the client to designers and contractors who may be bidding for the work so that the asbestos risks can be addressed.

**History**

The three types of asbestos that have found significant industrial uses are amosite (brown asbestos), chrysotile (white asbestos), and crocidolite (blue asbestos). None of these minerals are to be found in commercial quantities in the UK, with the bulk of the material that was used by industry imported from Canada or South Africa.

The physical and chemical properties of asbestos determined its uses and commercial value. The very fine fibres of chrysotile and crocidolite were ideal for textile products. Their thermal stability made the asbestos minerals useful in friction products and, together with their low thermal conductivity, in insulation materials.

Asbestos cements made with chrysotile asbestos were durable materials because of the chemical bonding of the lime with the surface of the fibres.

The use of asbestos was banned in Britain in 1999, but there are still a great deal of asbestos-containing materials in buildings and industrial plants.

Without delving too deep, up to this date chrysotile was by far the most abundant asbestos form in terms of production and usage (about 93 per cent).

It can be found in a wide variety of products, from yarn, rope, and textiles to cement, insulation boards, friction materials, gaskets, and thermoplastics.

Crocidolite had a similar widespread use, although the tendency was to use it in mixtures with other asbestos varieties. Amosite, because of its coarser nature, tended to find greater use in asbestos board and other rigid products. All three varieties may be found in all proportions in old laggings of pipes and boilers. Crocidolite was little used after about 1970, amosite after about 1980, and chrysotile after about 2000.

The uses of asbestos in building construction are divided into ten broad categories:

- Spray coatings and lagging
- Insulating board
- Ropes, yarn, and cloth
- Millboard, paper, and paper products
- Asbestos cement products
- Bitumen felts and coated metals
- Flooring materials
- Textured coatings and paints
- Mastic, sealants, putties, and adhesives
- Reinforced plastics

Spray coatings were used for anti-condensation and acoustic control or as fire protection on structural steel. They comprised a thin layer of cement and fibre mixture applied by a high-pressure spray.

The main fibre type used was amosite, although the other two main varieties may sometimes be found.

Laggings are found on boilers, pipes, and other items of plant (machinery). These pipe laggings may have been produced from pre-formed sections, by using boards or quilts, or trowelled on from a thick cement mixture, sometimes known as monkey dung.

Insulating boards were manufactured from cement or calcium silicate mixed with asbestos. They were produced to provide a low-density, low-cost, fire-resistant insulation and can be found in a wide variety of buildings, both commercial and domestic.

Asbestos yarns were used in the manufacture of asbestos cloth for fire protective clothing, gloves, and in fire blankets. They may also have been used in gaskets or packing materials.

Asbestos millboard and papers were generally used in fairly specialist applications, such as insulation of electrical equipment. They contain a high proportion of asbestos, and these products are easily damaged or abraded.

The fibre cement products produced with asbestos have had widespread use. They contain about 10 per cent asbestos; mostly chrysotile but some crocidolite or amosite were used prior to 1976. Fibre cement products differ from the insulating boards in their density, which is about two to three times higher.

The remaining applications - floor tiles, bitumen felts - have a much lower potential to release fibres and have generally not presented a great problem in use.

## Ecological Survey

With the exception of some very small householder applications, most development proposals will have the potential to impact local biodiversity in some way.

Usually, the purpose of a survey is to examine what habitats and species exist at the site **before** a planning application is submitted. This ensures the local planning authority (LPA) has sufficient information to make an informed decision that wildlife can be protected from injury or disturbance during development, and makes certain that there is no adverse impact on local biodiversity as a result of the development.

Ecological surveys identify the habitats and / or species that exist within an area at the time, which can be undertaken over a period to suit the nature of the survey. Most development proposals will have the potential to impact the local biodiversity of the site, through the direct loss of habitats, the reduction in the value of the habitat, or the ability of the habitat to support the species that depend on them. Early identification of any ecological constraints ensures that development proposals are not delayed, and appropriate mitigation or compensation is incorporated into the design phase.

### Purpose of ecological surveys

Undertaking ecological surveys will ensure that:

- The developer or applicant is aware of any ecological constraints at an early stage.
- The development can be designed to minimise impact on biodiversity.

- Any legally protected species (European or British) or notable species are identified so that the development can avoid or minimise impact upon them.
- The design of mitigation and enhancement measures will be appropriate to the site and surrounding area.
- The local planning authority can consider all the relevant material considerations whilst determining an application.

An ecological survey can be the subject of a planning condition. This can include:

- Assessment of the ecological value of the site and how this will change post-development.
- Recommendations for the protection of ecological features and mitigating impact.
- Recommendations on how to enhance the site for ecology.
- Assessment of the long-term impact on biodiversity, which can include a management plan for the development.

The typical ecological surveys that may be required in support of a planning application or as part of an environmental impact assessment include:

- Extended Phase I habitat survey (baseline assessment that determines that broad habitat types within a site and the potential for the site to support protected / notable species).

- Botanical survey (including National Vegetation Classification -NVC)
- The presence of Bats
- Badgers
- Dormice
- Water voles
- Otters
- Reptiles
- Birds
- Great crested newts
- Natterjack toads
- Smooth snakes
- Invertebrates

## Archaeological Survey

It is not outside the realms of possibility that you may be required to conduct an archaeological survey. The introduction of a number of government guidance notes on archaeology and planning has resulted in most development proposals being checked by local planning authorities. Large or small, urban, greenfield or brownfield – any development can come into conflict with archaeology and the need to contend with the presence of archaeological remains.

Archaeological intervention required by a planning authority can range from a pre-application assessment, observation, and recording during construction, through various stages and scales of pre-development excavation and scientific analysis. Some local planning authorities now request archaeological surveys of standing buildings, listed or otherwise. In some instances, an application may be refused because of the perceived importance of the archaeology. The implications can be expensive in both time and money.

One of the most significant aspects introduced by planning policies could be the need to carry out archaeological evaluations **before** a planning application is determined. These evaluations can range from a desktop study through to physical examination of a percentage of the site proposed for development. Reluctance to provide an evaluation can result in planning permission being refused.

Where the evaluation determines that important archaeological remains exist on a site, it will normally be necessary to devise a means of protecting the archaeology to gain planning permission. This does not automatically mean large-scale, expensive archaeological excavation.

Early advice from a suitably experienced planning archaeologist can identify more cost effective design solutions. Archaeological sites can be preserved by their incorporation into open space, absorbed into landscaping, or even buried beneath a sealing layer. Use of appropriate foundations can minimise the amount of ground disturbance and thereby minimise the need for archaeological recording. These are all decisions that need to be made early in the design stage.

**Typical requirements**

A **desktop study** involves the examination and evaluation of local, regional, or national archaeological records. It may include aerial photographs, old maps, and published records, and a rapid surface inspection of the site. It should produce a written report and recommendations for the local planning authority.

A **field evaluation** may be requested. This may include a geophysical survey: a technique that can detect buried features without disturbing the ground; and a sampling excavation: usually a series of small-scale trenches or test pits dug by an archaeological contractor. A field evaluation should be integrated with other geotechnical work.

A **Grampian condition** is used to impose a scheme of archaeological recording on a development. It requires the scheme to be submitted to and agreed by the local planning authority, and the recording to be implemented before development can commence.

A **watching brief** requires the presence of a trained archaeologist on-site to record features as they are revealed during construction. It should be organised in a way that minimises delay in case of other site works.

An **excavation** may range from the detailed examination and recording of a part of a site through to its total excavation. It is the most costly element of any archaeological intervention.

The **post-excavation analysis** involves the detailed scientific analysis of the results of an excavation.

Where rich deposits are identified, particularly waterlogged remains, it can cost as much again as the excavation.

The publication of important findings may require both scientific and general works to be commissioned, and care and long-term curation of the archive will be required.

## Surface Water and Flood Risk Survey

National and local planning policy considers the impact and implications of flooding on new developments (and redevelopment), since in recent years, the UK has experienced heavy rainfall, strong winds, storm surges, and high tides combined together to cause widespread flooding. With climate change predicted to cause more frequent high-intensity rainfall events and rising sea levels, flooding is likely to become an increasing problem.

Ever increasingly, the Environment Agency is requesting (by means of conditions of planning consent) that a flood management plan / flood warning and evacuation plan be prepared for developments located within areas at risk of flooding.

### SUR 1 - Surface water

Although no longer a mandatory requirement of the Code for Sustainable Homes, it is strongly recommended that should a planning condition be imposed, this be considered as part of the investigation process in order to ensure that the conditioned elements can be feasibly achieved.

Under SUR 1, a report must be prepared (by an appropriately qualified professional) in order to demonstrate that there will be no increase in the peak rate and volume of surface water runoff from the redeveloped site (when compared with the existing situation, including an allowance for climate change), and that there will be no flooding to the dwelling should the local drainage system fail.

The level of detail required in the report is dependent upon the extent of hardstanding areas at the existing and redeveloped site.

Where redevelopment of the site results in an increase in hardstanding areas, it must be demonstrated that:

- Surface water flows (the peak rate of runoff) from the site will not increase over the lifetime of the development, including an allowance for climate change.

- If soil conditions are favourable, the preferred method is through infiltration techniques (such as soakaways or permeable paving).

- There will be no increase in the volume of surface water runoff leaving the site.

Any additional volume must be prevented from leaving the site by using infiltration techniques. If ground conditions are not favourable, then other source control Sustainable Drainage System (SuDS) techniques must be considered (such as rainwater harvesting).

If this approach for addressing any additional volume of surface water runoff is not feasible, and full justification for this is provided in the report, then it must be demonstrated that:

Surface water flows will be restricted in accordance with the flow rates as detailed in the CSH technical guide - it should be noted that this could result in large storage volume requirements.

The SUR 1 report must also include a flood risk / consequences assessment in accordance with NPPF (England) / TAN 15 (Wales), to confirm the risk of flooding from all sources.

**SUR 2 - Flood risk**

The aim of SUR 2 is to promote housing development in low flood risk areas, or to take measures to reduce the impact of flooding on houses built in areas with medium or high risk of flooding.

**Evidence requirements:**

A flood risk assessment (FRA) (England) or flood consequences assessment (FCA) (Wales) is required in order to confirm the risk of flooding to the site from all sources, including:

Fluvial and tidal - The Environment Agency flood maps provide a general indication of the flood zone classification of a site. Flood zones only relate to fluvial and tidal flood risk and do not take into account the presence of any flood defences such as:

Groundwater
Sewers and highway drains
Surface water
Artificial bodies (including canals and reservoirs)

For developments situated in areas of medium or high annual probability of flooding where finished floor levels of the dwelling are appropriately raised (generally at least 600 mm above modelled flood levels) and appropriate flood resistance and resilient construction techniques are incorporated, it must also be demonstrated that safe access and egress can be provided.

## Noise Survey

If you are building near a large road, railway, or airport, it is more than likely that planners will condition you with an acoustic survey.

Noise is often a concern for residential developments particularly in urban and suburban areas. The local planning authority can often place pre-commencement conditions relating to noise on a residential planning application.

The following areas relating to noise created by the site are often considered:

- Noise and vibration from construction works
- Noise created by the residential development
- Existing noise levels affecting future habitants of the residential development
- Noise impact caused by plant and equipment associated with the development

All residential development must comply with Approved Document E of the Building Regulations, which sets out the acoustic design criteria for residential buildings.

A noise survey is generally requested during a planning application where noise is of concern to the future habitants of the proposed development. The purpose of the noise survey is to establish the existing environmental noise levels at the proposed site and assess the suitability of the development.

On the flip side, noise impact assessments are generally required when a new noise source has been proposed for an existing area. The assessment will determine the level of impact the proposed noise source will have on the existing noise climate.

To carry out a noise impact assessment, a noise survey is required to establish the existing noise levels in the area and at nearby noise-sensitive locations. The proposed noise source(s) is then compared to the existing noise levels to determine the level of impact. Depending on the noise source in question, there is a considerable body of legislation and standards that provides guidance on the level of impact.

Typically, a noise survey is carried out over a 24-hour period. The local planning authority may request a longer surveying period depending on the noise sources of concern. Once the environmental noise levels of the site have been established, a façade assessment of the proposed residential building(s) is carried out to ensure internal noise levels are suitable. Noise break-in calculations are then carried out in accordance with British Standard 8233:1999 *Sound Insulation and Noise Reduction for Building - Code of Practice* (BS8233:1999) to predict the likely internal noise levels within a typical dwelling.

A planning report is then provided with details of the noise survey and resultant measured noise levels for the site. Details of the façade assessment are also included within the report along with the required glazing and ventilation attenuation specifications to achieve suitable internal noise levels. This will be suitable for submission to the local planning authority to release any planning conditions relating to environmental noise.

Alternatively, a pre-commencement condition could be imposed requesting details of measures to be taken to protect from a known noise source, such as under a flight path.

These measures can be in the form of high-spec glazing or insulation, and often since open windows could be an issue, the use of Mechanical Ventilated Heat Recovery (MVHR).

# 16

# Party Wall

Not all prospective self-builders realise that if building on or near the boundary of the construction site, then you need a party wall agreement in place. The majority think that the legislation relates to actual 'works on a party wall', and thus think that, say, if constructing a new house inside the boundary, then an agreement is not necessary. You could be wrong!

Since the whole process can be quite involved, I will give you a synopsis of requirements and procedures – this information is not exhaustive.

## The Party Wall act and Notices:

The Party Wall etc. Act 1996 provides a framework for preventing and resolving disputes in relation to party walls, boundary walls, and excavations near neighbouring buildings.

A building owner proposing to start work covered by the Act must give adjoining owners notice of their intentions in the way set down in the Act. Adjoining owners can agree or disagree with what is proposed. Where they disagree, the Act provides a mechanism for resolving disputes.

The Act covers:

- New building on or against the boundary of two properties.
- Work on an existing party wall or party structure.
- Excavation near and below the foundation level of neighbouring buildings.

- Building a new wall on or at the boundary of two properties.
- Cutting into a party wall.
- Making a party wall taller, shorter, or deeper.
- Removing chimney breasts from a party wall.
- Knocking down and rebuilding a party wall.
- Digging below the foundation level of a neighbour's property.

You must find out whether any of the above work falls within the Act. If it does, you must notify all adjoining owners. If work starts without a notice being given, an adjoining owner can seek to stop the work through a court injunction or can seek other legal redress.

Understanding the principles of the Act is often helpful if owners think of themselves as joint owners of the whole party wall rather than the sole owner of half or part of it.

Let's explore the different scenarios:

**1. Work which has a direct effect on a party wall (or other party structure):**

The list of works a building owner has the right to undertake but would have a direct effect on a party wall and, therefore, is covered under the act are given under Section 2(2) of the act. I have enlisted them with some common examples:

(a) 'To underpin, thicken or raise a party structure, a party fence wall, or an external wall which belongs to the building owner and is built against a party structure or party fence wall' - *This section includes the condition that a building owner can increase the height of a party wall, say, as part of a loft conversion or to add an extra floor to a building or to underpin the whole width of a party wall which has suffered from subsidence.*

(b) 'To make good, repair, or demolish and rebuild, a party structure or party fence wall in a case where such work is necessary on account of defect or want of repair of the structure or wall' - *Where a party wall has become defective, either owner can take the initiative and serve notice to have it repaired or re-built. The costs of the work are split according to the use that the owners make of the wall and responsibility for the defect or lack of repair.*

Sub-sections (c) and (d) can be ignored for works on residential properties

(e) 'To demolish a party structure which is of insufficient strength or height for the purposes of any intended building of the building owner and to rebuild it of sufficient strength or height for the said purposes (including rebuilding to a lesser height or thickness where the rebuilt structure is of sufficient strength and height for the purposes of any adjoining owner)' – *This right would only be exercised as a last resort, as the costs would be considerable; including the payment of compensation to the adjoining owner for disturbance and inconvenience. Most designers / engineers would explore alternative options first.*

(f) 'To cut into a party structure for any purpose (which may be or include the purpose of inserting a damp proof course)' – *This right is most commonly exercised by a building owner cutting pockets in to a party wall to insert beams. It also covers the insertion of flashings and damp-proofing works that involve drilling or cutting into the party wall.*

(g) 'To cut away from a party wall, party fence wall, external wall or boundary wall any footing or any projecting chimney breast, jamb or flue, or other projection on or over the land of the building owner in order to erect, raise or underpin any such wall or for any other purpose' – *This section covers the demolition of chimney breasts attached to a party wall but also gives the building owner the right to cut away other projections from the party wall, such as footings, if they impede his building work.*

(h) 'To cut away or demolish parts of any wall or building of an adjoining owner overhanging the land of the building owner or overhanging a party wall, to the extent that it is necessary to cut away or demolish the parts to enable a vertical wall to be erected or raised against the wall or building of the adjoining owner' – *In practice, this relates to items such as rainwater goods, soffits, and fascias or coping stones which will be in the way of a building owner wanting to raise his wall . The building owner has the duty to make good any damage.*

(j) 'To cut into the wall of an adjoining owner's building in order to insert a flashing or other weather-proofing of a wall erected against that wall' – *If a building owner constructs an extension alongside an adjoining owner's existing extension, it is likely that a small gap will remain. It would normally be in the interests of both owners to waterproof the gap with a flashing. If that flashing has to be cut into the adjoining owner's wall, this section gives the building owner the right to do just that.*

(k) 'To execute any other necessary works incidental to the connection of a party structure with the premises adjoining it' – *In practical terms, this section is only likely to be used in residential situations where a building owner wants to re-build his property but leave the party wall in place; it may then be necessary to form a more permanent connection between the party wall and the adjoining structure and to attach the new building to the existing party wall.*

(l) 'To raise a party fence wall, or to raise such a wall for use as a party wall, and to demolish a party fence wall and rebuild it as a party fence wall or as a party wall' – *A party fence wall is effectively a garden wall which is in shared ownership – they are commonly found between period properties; particularly those with back additions that have windows to the side.*

(m) 'Subject to the provisions of Section 11(7), to reduce, or to demolish and rebuild, a party wall or party fence wall to -

(i) a height of not less than two metres where the wall is not used by an adjoining owner

(ii) to any greater extent than a boundary wall; or a height currently enclosed upon by the building of an adjoining owner *This section is aimed at a building owner who wants to reduce the height of a party wall or a shared garden wall down to a height of no less than 2 metres so long as it doesn't compromise the adjoining owner's building. If both owners are in agreement, the wall can be removed altogether.*

(n) 'To expose a party wall or party structure hitherto enclosed subject to providing adequate weathering' - *The purpose of this section is really to protect an adjoining owner where a building owner plans to remove part or all of his structure and, as a result, expose the party wall. It may be necessary to protect the newly exposed wall with felt and battens; if the exposure is temporary, or if it is to be permanently exposed, a more permanent solution, such as rendering or re-pointing, may be required.*

The notice period for works under Section 2 of the Act is two calendar months.

**2. Excavation close to an adjoining owner's building:**
It surprises many building owners that they must serve a notice to their neighbour, even though the trench they plan to dig will be entirely on their own land. The reason, of course, is that excavating close to any structure carries a risk that the foundations of that structure will be compromised and movement will occur.

This type of work is covered by Section 6 of the Act and can be divided into two parts. Here, I have given the relevant text from the Act together with a sketch, which I hope will clarify the description.

**Section 6(1),** where:

(a) a building owner proposes to excavate, or excavate for and erect a building or structure, within a distance of three metres measured horizontally from any part of a building or structure of an adjoining owner; and

(b) any part of the proposed excavation, building or structure will within those three metres extend to a lower level than the level of the bottom of the foundations of the building or structure of the adjoining owner.

3 Metre Notice

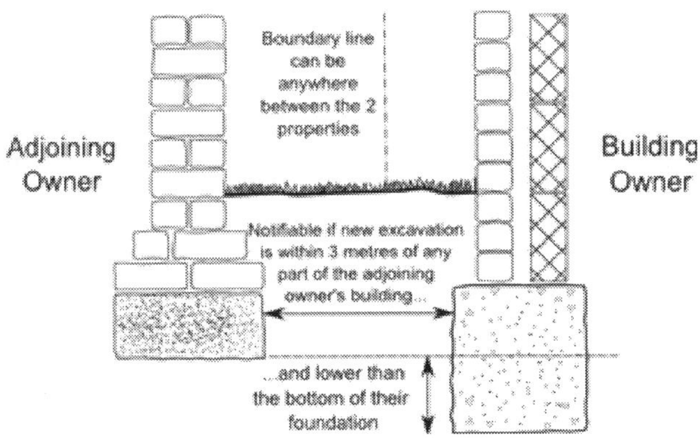


**Section 6(2),** where:

(a) a building owner proposes to excavate, or excavate for and erect a building or structure, within a distance of six metres measured horizontally from any part of a building or structure of an adjoining owner; and

(b) any part of the proposed excavation, building or structure will within those six metres meet a plane drawn downwards in the direction of the excavation, building or structure of the building owner at an angle of 45 degrees to the horizontal from the line formed by the intersection of the plane of the level of the bottom of the foundations of the building or structure of the adjoining owner with the plane of the external face of the external wall of the building or structure of the adjoining owner.

6 Metre Notice

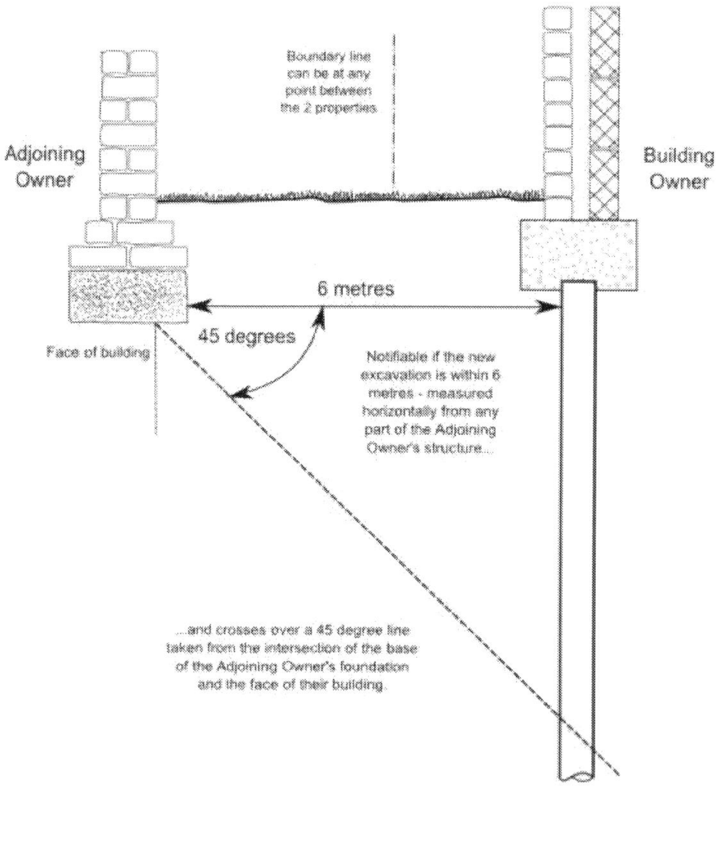


The notice period for excavation work which comes within the scope of the Act is one calendar month.

**3. Construction of a new wall at the line of junction between two properties:**
This category covers the construction of new walls at the line of junction, that is, the boundary line between two properties in different ownership. The new wall may be built up to the boundary line but wholly on the land of the building owner or astride the boundary line – with part of it on each owner's side. If the adjoining owner refuses consent, then the wall must be built wholly on the building owner's side. The construction of a new wall at the line of junction is covered under Section 1 of the Act.

A building owner might want to carry out work detailed under this section of the Act for two practical reasons:

1. To maximise the width of a rear extension:

If the flank walls of a new extension can be built astride the boundary, then a few extra square feet of internal floor space will be gained. It should be noted that new walls built astride the boundary under this section of the Act will be defined as party walls and may be enclosed upon by the adjoining owner at a later stage (subject to serving notice and contributing towards the cost of building the wall).

2. To replace an existing boundary wall, fence, or hedge with a party wall or party fence wall:

This is less common, and the motivation will generally be to provide additional privacy or to overcome the maintenance that is required with fences and hedges.

The notice period for building a new wall at the line of junction is one calendar month. Procedures differ based on works under Sections 2 and 6 of the Act in that there is no automatic dissent to a notice after 14 days.

If the wall that the building owner wishes to construct is wholly on his own land, and he has had no response to his notice after one calendar month has passed, he is free to proceed.

**How do I inform the adjoining owner or owners?**

It is obviously best to discuss your planned work fully with the adjoining owners before you (or your professional adviser on your behalf) give notice, in writing, about what you plan to do. If you have already ironed out possible snags with your neighbours, this should mean that they will readily give consent in response to your notice. You do not need to appoint a professional adviser to give the notice on your behalf. However, if you do, you should satisfy yourself in terms of the experience and professional qualifications of your adviser.

Whilst there is no official form for giving notice under the Act, your notice will need to include the following details:

- Your own name and address (joint owners must all be named – for example, Mr A & Mrs B Owner)
- The address of the building to be worked on (this may be different from your main or current address)
- A full description of what you propose to do (it may be helpful to include plans, and you must do so with respect to excavation works, but you must still describe the works)
- When you propose to start (which must not be before the relevant notice period has elapsed).

The notice should be dated, and it is advisable to include a clear statement that it is a notice under the provisions of the Act.

You may deliver the notice to the adjoining owner(s) in person or send it by post. Alternatively, if you do not know the name of the owner and / or the property is rented out, you may address the notice to 'The Owner', adding the address of the premises, and deliver it to a person on the premises, or, if the neighbouring property is empty, fix it to a conspicuous part of the premises.

**How long in advance do I have to serve the notice?**

In the case of works to the actual party wall, the notice period is at least two months before the planned start date for work on the party wall.

In the case of excavation near the neighbouring building, the notice period is one month.

The adjoining owner may agree to allow works to start earlier but is not obliged to even when agreement on the works is reached. The notice is only valid for a year, so do not serve it too long before you wish to start.

**What happens after I serve notice?**

A person who receives a notice about intended work may:

- Give his consent in writing, or
- Refuse to consent to the works proposed (the dispute resolution procedure then comes into play), or

- Do nothing. If, after a period of 14 days from the service of your notice, the person receiving the notice has done nothing, a dispute is deemed to have arisen.

As suggested above, your notice should not come as a surprise. If you have already ironed out possible snags with your neighbours, this should mean that they will more readily give consent in response to your notice. It should be noted that where consent is given, you are not relieved of your obligations under the Act – for example, to avoid unnecessary inconvenience or to provide temporary protection for adjacent buildings and property where necessary. The notice of consent is simply confirmation that, at that time, there is nothing 'in dispute'.

### What happens if I receive a counter-notice?

A person who receives notice about intended work may, within one month, give a counter-notice setting out what additional or modified work he would like to be carried out for his own benefit, accompanied by all necessary particulars. However, a person who receives a notice and intends to give a counter-notice should let the building owner know within 14 days.

If you receive a counter-notice, you must respond to it within 14 days. Otherwise, a dispute is deemed to have arisen

### What if I cannot reach agreement with the adjoining owners on the work to be done to the party wall?

The best way to settle any point of difference is by friendly discussion with your neighbour. Agreements should always be put in writing.

If you cannot reach agreement with the adjoining owners, the next best thing is to agree with them on appointing what the Act calls an 'Agreed Surveyor' to draw up an 'award'.

The surveyor must be a person agreed between the owners to act. Alternatively, each owner can appoint a surveyor to draw up the award together. The two appointed surveyors will select a third surveyor (who would be called in only if the two appointed surveyors cannot agree or either of the owners or either surveyor calls upon the third surveyor to make an award). In all cases, surveyors appointed or selected under the dispute resolution procedure of the Act must consider the interests and rights of both owners and draw up an award impartially.

The duty of the surveyor is to resolve matters in dispute in a fair and practical way. Where separate surveyors are appointed by each owner, the surveyors must liaise with their appointing owners and put forward the respective owners' preferred outcome.

However, beyond that, the surveyors do not act as representatives for respective owners. They must always act consistently with the terms of the Act to reach a fair and impartial award.

**Whom can I appoint as a surveyor in the event of a dispute?**
The term 'surveyor' under the Act can include any person who is not a party to the matter.

This means that you can appoint almost anyone you like to act in this capacity. However, the person should not have already been engaged to supervise the building work. The surveyor should also have a good knowledge of construction and of procedures under the Act.

Some people are obviously more suitable than others. You may wish to look for a qualified building professional with some experience or knowledge of party wall matters.

You cannot act as a surveyor for yourself.

**What does the surveyor do?**

The surveyor (or surveyors) will settle the matter by making an 'award' (also known as a 'party wall award').

This is a document which:

- Sets out the work that will be carried out.
- Says when and how the work is to be carried out (for example, to limit continuous periods of time when excessively noisy work can be carried out).
- Specifies any additional work required (for example, necessary protection to prevent damage).
- Often contains a record of the condition of the adjoining property before the work begins (so that any damage to the adjoining land or buildings can be properly attributed and made good).
- Allows access for the surveyor(s) to inspect the works while they're going on as may be necessary (to see that they are in accordance with the award).

It is a good idea to keep a copy of the award with your property deeds when the works are completed.

### Who pays the surveyor's fees?

Usually, the building owner will pay all costs associated with drawing up the award including the adjoining owner's surveyor's fees, if the works are solely for the building owner's benefit. However, in certain circumstances where work is necessary due to defect or in need of repair, the adjoining owner may have to pay costs. In these circumstances, the costs are split based on the use each owner has of the structure or wall concerned; the responsibility for the defect or need for repair also arises if more than one owner makes use of the structure or wall concerned.

The surveyor (or surveyors) will decide who pays the fees for drawing up the award and for checking that the work has been carried out in accordance with the award.

### How much will a surveyor cost?

Surveyor's fees are a matter for individual surveyors. There are no set charges. It is for clients to negotiate fees with the surveyor(s).

### Is the surveyor's award final?

The award is final and binding unless it is rescinded or modified by a county court on appeal. Each owner has 14 days from service of the award on them to appeal to the county court against the award.

An appeal should not be undertaken lightly, and an unsuccessful appellant may incur an award of costs against them. An owner considering an appeal may well wish to seek legal advice.

# 17

# Utility Services

The requirements and planning of existing and new incoming utility services is often underestimated, especially in terms of timing. I cannot emphasise enough the importance of getting the ball rolling with this as early as possible.

Bear in mind that water and electricity will also be needed during the build.

## Demolishing an Existing Property

If you are taking down an existing house, then all services must be isolated and disconnected before any demo works can commence. Now that may seem like an obvious thing to be doing, but the mechanics and timing can seriously affect your programming and costing if not attended to correctly.

## Water

Any pipe on your side of the stop cock located at the boundary is your responsibility. So as long as you stick to fairly easy guidelines, you do not need input from your water company.

If you are on a metered supply, where the meter in its underground chamber would usually be found just outside the curtilage of the plot, it is a fairly straightforward exercise to isolate the existing supply by shutting it off in the meter pit. Unless the house to be demolished has had a service pipe recently replaced, the existing pipe will be steel, so it cannot really be used moving forward. Expose the pipe down the side of the meter and disconnect it; then lay a blue poly pipe underground from the meter as a temporary supply to a stand pipe which is best located well away from any future works. I will address site layout in a different chapter.

The new permanent supply pipe will be laid as part of the groundworks but in a trench min 750 mm deep from the meter to the new position in the building. If passing through / under the foundations or floor, the pipe must be laid in a flexible duct so it can, in theory, be pulled out and replaced at a later date if necessary. For this reason, since ducting is not a particularly expensive commodity, I would always recommend laying the duct for its entire length back to the meter.

Bearing in mind that you are dealing with an existing supply, timing is not a major issue, as you are totally in control.

## Gas

The gas will need to be disconnected at the boundary and the meter removed, which will more than likely involve two different organisations. To clarify, one organisation provides the gas mains, pipes, and so on in roads, and another (many to choose from) will actually sell you the gas and provide the meter.

To have the service pipe disconnected is a fairly straightforward exercise, which involves establishing the infrastructure provider, filling in a form (often online), paying a fee, and waiting a few weeks.

The removal of the meter can be a bit more involved subject in relation to whose name the account is in and who is actually charging for the gas, which is not always obvious. All properties have a Meter Point Reference Number (MPRN) which will tell any supplier who owns the meter. You then contact them and have the meter removed. Little tip here: take a photo of the meter in position, showing its last reading before it is removed.

To then organise a new gas supply, you will start the procedure from scratch, with a new service pipe and new meter from your chosen supplier.

**Electric**

The existing supply and meter will need to be removed from the building prior to demo works, and you will need a temporary supply during the construction phase. The two can usually be done with one application.

Whilst you have a similar circumstance regarding the infrastructure and the meter being owned by two separate organisations, you can have the existing supply moved, with the meter, by the relevant electric company. They will also, as a separate job, reinstate to the new position once the new build is at the relevant stage. Once again, careful planning of ducting will pay dividends later.

## New Build

### Water

Out of the three main services, water is notoriously the longest to organise.

First, you apply to your water company by filling in a form and sending the relevant information. This can often involve a soil survey if it is at all likely that you have ground conditions that will require a barrier pipe. This is a special quality of water pipe, the normal one being the blue Medium-Density Polythene (MDPE) pipe and barrier pipe being MDPE blue with a brown stripe running along it for identification. If there is any form of contamination in the ground - and this could mean the likes of Radon, which I will cover in a separate chapter - barrier pipe will be specified by the water company and you will not have any choice in the matter. If the water company says it must be barrier, then barrier it will be, so make sure that you install the correct one. Whilst this type of pipe is not hugely more expensive than the standard blue, not all merchants will have it or its fittings on the shelf.

You will be asked if you require the connection for building water, which of course you will. This can be achieved by either the temporary stand pipe as above, or to the eventual new position, but either will be required to be laid in a trench of the correct depth and be either covered in soft sand or ducted. This is where the timing comes in because you are going to need water almost from the word go, but you will not get a connection until paperwork is in place and the pipe (with necessary non-return stopcock, fixed to a post, and so on) in its open trench has been inspected. For this reason, it is best to have a temporary standpipe, just inside the boundary, which can easily be installed, inspected, and connected without disruption to the remainder of the works at early stages. You can then lay the new permanent pipe later on at your convenience and without the drama of leaving the trench open for inspection.

Some water companies – Thames Water, for example – will charge a fee at application stage, which is taken into consideration when paying for the eventual connection fee.

Remember also to indicate whether or not you will be connecting your foul drainage to the main sewer infrastructure, as this will affect how much you pay both at connection stage and from that point onwards, with your bills. Approximately half of your water bill is for clean water coming in and the other half for foul drainage going out.

So if, for example, you are not connecting to the main sewer and are using a septic tank or other waste treatment, you should not be paying the water company for this waste service.

Once you have your quote back and have paid the invoice, slow wheels will be put in motion for survey, inspection and eventual connection.

**Gas**

Gas is probably the easiest to organise initially but quite involved mechanically.

In theory, the new service pipe will be connected to the existing nearest main by the gas infrastructure company, which could be over the other side of a road or further, and laid in a trench (usually excavated by you inside the boundary) to the meter point. Some will allow ducting under certain circumstances and some will not – see my note further in the chapter regarding types of ducting. Likewise, some will allow a groundwork contractor to lay the pipe in a duct at the early stages.

None will come and lay the pipe on site whilst there is scaffold erected, so consider the logistics carefully.

## Electric

Since you will be needing electric virtually from the word go, most providers will let you install a temporary supply in a cabinet, which can be adapted at a later stage into the permanent supply. Once again, forward thinking with ducting will make life easier later.

A little note regarding gas and electric meter cabinets of the type which are designed to be built flush into the external wall: these 'cavity' boxes work fine with masonry construction that have a 100 mm cavity or more.

However, if you are building timber frame with a brick skin and 50 mm cavity, the cabinets will be too deep by about 15 mm which just works if you are using a block skin and render. Other than that, you will need to cut the timber frame panel to allow the box to sink in enough, which is not always a satisfactory answer. Also with masonry, subject to which cavity insulation you are using, you could have a cold bridge issue if you need to cut the insulation to get the box in flush. These types of boxes, although tidy, are becoming more of a design consideration as time goes by.

On the subject of ducting, there are different types and colours of duct for each different utility pipe or cable. Most come in a coil, and is best to stick to the correct duct to avoid tears later on when a utility engineer refuses to connect / lay their incoming as you have not provided the correct duct.

As a rule, water is laid in a blue duct, which is normally perforated.

Electricity is laid in black, which is rigid or semi-rigid and not perforated.

Gas has to be laid in perforated yellow duct.

Telephone uses grey, which usually comes in the form of lengths of pipe rather than coils.

Media (cable telly) uses green.

It is always good practice to provide a strong draw chord inside the duct that can be used later to pull the cable through.

# 18

# Planning the Logistics and Layout of the Site

Now it is more than likely that as part of a planning condition, you have had to mark on a drawing where materials will be kept, where vehicles will be offloaded, and the position of, say, welfare facilities.

This is more of a box-ticking exercise initiated mainly by the highways officer to demonstrate that delivery vehicles and site operative vans have been thought about in their relationship to the site and surrounding roads. Can a delivery lorry be unloaded within the site? Can vehicles turn around on site without reversing onto the highway? Where will contractors park without clogging up the local roads and keeping mud off the roads?

To digress on the subject of mud on the road, nothing is a more sure fire way of having the Local Authority highways officer breathing down your neck and generally making your life a misery than mud from the site being deposited on the highway by truck and plant movement.

Whilst as part of this exercise you will be roughly indicating the location of certain items, a lot more thought needs to go into this for the mechanics of the site, with timing probably the most important.

Let's think about the ingredients of site logistics, which more often than not, have a relationship with how long each item would be in place, but also be influenced by the confines of the site itself.

Although there are no real rules regarding positions, a well thought out discipline will benefit the site and the build itself.

## Welfare and Storage

**Portaloo**: Although this is obviously movable to suit changing conditions, it needs to be placed in a position where it can be serviced easily each week.

**Storage**: If you are going to be bringing a storage container to site, chances are, it will be there for quite some time; so you need to think carefully about where to put it. Although the container delivery trucks usually have very long reaching hiabs (lorry-mounted cranes), will the easily reached position at the beginning of the works still be equally achievable at the end when some of the hardscaping works are complete? Sure it can be moved, but bear in mind that to deliver and collect (therefore, to move) costs more than the hire. Make sure also that you do not position it where trenches need to be dug during the course of the build.

It is often worth waiting until certain works are completed before bringing several tons of steel containers to the site.

## Materials Storage

The positioning of materials can either save or cost money in a build. Generally, you want to have them dropped as near as possible to where they will be used, but without getting in the way of other materials and trades. A full load (15–18 packs) of bricks takes up a huge amount of space and needs to be timed to perfection.

The storage and, therefore, the amount of materials on site at any one time is totally dictated by the size of the plot and the stage of the build. There are clear financial advantages to being able to have direct to-site full loads of, say, blocks delivered as opposed to a few packs at a time from the merchant, but you would need lots of space, and not all sites have that luxury. On a confined site, timing is crucial. You do not want roof trusses kicking around whilst you are trying to find room for the next load of bricks or blocks. There are other reasons that you would not want trusses on site too early, and that is that they will deteriorate or get damaged. The best time a for a truss delivery is the day before they are lifted, no matter how much room you have. This leads to another consideration: if materials are kicking around on site for too long, you run the risk of them becoming damaged, lost, or stolen.

Can the job afford a forklift at certain times? This would mean that the aforementioned blocks could be stored well way from where they are required. Just bear in mind that the forklift itself requires a lot of space to manoeuvre.

A quick note on the subject of forklifts and pallets - quite often, materials are brought to site not on pallets but placed by the lorry onto pallets to be lifted later by the forklift.

Make sure that the pallets are placed the correct way round to enable the forks to get into the slots in the pallet.

This is a very simple thing to get right but a headache if it goes wrong.

Whilst we are on the subject of pallets - which are an absolute nuisance at the best of times - quite often, the pallets themselves are chargeable items. In theory, these can be redeemed, but in practice, it becomes tedious to do so. Once you have accumulated a few non-chargeable pallets (and believe me you will), look into having certain materials delivered without pallets and dropped on to your own pallets. By the end of an average new build, you could have acquired as many as 50 pallets (many charged at £16 a pop), which can be a real pain to dispose of. More often than not, you cannot burn anything on site; and the last thing you want to be doing is filling up a couple of skips at £300 each time with leftover pallets.

## Vehicles

You have to consider the contractors' vans (perhaps as many as four at any one time), delivery lorries, and plant such as forklift or cranes.

On the subject of craneage, even a small crane takes up a lot of space, and this space is controlled by what is being lifted and to where. Even a small 25-tonne crane costs a lot to hire (probably £500 per day), so you want to be making sure that the correct sized crane can be sited in exactly the right position for the shortest possible time. Another point when deciding where a crane would sit is to consider the footprint of the scaffold and its impedance implications when deciding where the crane can lift from.

That applies generally to all other planning – the scaffold will take up approximately 1500 mm all round, not including loading bays.

The need to get the contractors' vehicles on site speaks for itself, but some trades – plumbers, for example – need more regular access to their vans than others, so a priority system could be needed.

Delivery lorries, according to what they are delivering, require different facilities. In most cases, the lorry will want to offload to the side with its hiab, sometimes to the rear and almost never over the front of the cab. Local authorities, especially highways, get very tetchy if loading / unloading takes place on the highway unless absolutely necessary. I touched on it earlier, but if it is likely that due to site conditions it will be necessary for unloading to take place on the road, expect them to demand some form of document in the form of a Construction Method Statement, as mentioned in the pre-commence planning conditions chapter.

## Waste

Now for the purpose of this chapter, I am not writing about the environmental and sustainability side of waste management and disposal. I am writing this next section on the practicalities of waste at the site logistics level.

Waste disposal takes on a totally different dimension in case of a renovation rather than a new build; therefore, the type and amount of waste has different requirements and places on site.

## Renovation

There are fundamentally three types of waste: inert, non-inert, and specialist.

To break it down to its most basic explanation, inert is material that will not rot, such as dirt and rubble that can be taken away and used for straightforward build up at another location. Non-inert is the remainder of the waste.

Coupled with this, there are several different methods of disposal according to the quantities involved.

Let's say, for example, you are renovating a building that also requires an element of extending. You are likely to be stripping out the interior of doors, kitchens, carpets, wallpaper, and so on, this will go into the non-inert pile. I will get to how best to dispose these in a minute.

Then you knock down walls and dig a foundation – this is inert waste.

So far as the non-inert waste is concerned, waste disposal would usually take the form of skips, which, because of the ever-growing landfill tax, are an expensive and often underestimated commodity. Skips would usually come in the form of 6 yard upwards to 14 yard. The rule of thumb here is generally, the larger the skip, the more you are concerned with bulk rather than weight. Quite simply, there is a limit as to the amount of weight that the skip lorry can pick up. Apart from a 6 yard, the price of this type of skip usually carries a maximum weight with an additional sum if exceeded. That means you should be careful when filling the skip; weight aside, diligent stacking of materials in skips can avoid gaps of valuable space that in turn results in additional cost.

If you have the space and requirement, roll-on-roll-off (ROLO) skips are more cost-effective.

These are brought to site on a totally different lorry (requiring a lot more manoeuvre room) and can be hired as a 20 yard or even 40 yard, the latter being the size of a decent steel container with doors on the back and the roof cut off. Costs of these ROLO skips vary according to the agreed weight before penalties, but generally, if you have the need and the space, they are cost-effective.

Back to our site logistics – because the size of the skip determines the space it takes up, remember to factor that the lorry needs to be able to set it down and pick it up. Having said that, the position designated for the skip(s) can be a movable feast according to the stage of the job.

With the inert waste, we have an additional method of disposal, and that is the grab lorry.

Assuming you have the quantity (grab lorries take on average 14 yard), this method is by far the most cost-effective way to dispose of inert waste. The cost of a grab load will usually compare to a 6-yard skip, and since a 6 yard is the only size that you can fully load with this type of material due to the weight, you do the maths! Sometimes, it is still cost-effective if you do not have a full load.

However, you need the space to accumulate the material until you have a full load, and this space needs to be factored in on your site layout. A grab lorry loads from the side, so you need to also have the space for the truck to sit whilst loading. A small consideration with all waste disposal trucks is that they require quite a lot of headroom, so keep this space away from trees and cables.

A word of warning when using a grab lorry. This is only to be used for dirt and clean hardcore.

If you start mixing in anything not deemed inert (you have taken down a lath and plaster ceiling – the plaster is inert, the wooden laths are not) and put the lot on the inert pile, this then becomes mixed waste and the cost goes up to eye-watering numbers.

One last aspect of waste, and that the consideration for any specialist requirements. Putting aside any obligatory waste management plans, it is entirely possible that your local skip company will restrict what is considered mixed waste. Some, for example, will not allow plasterboard off-cuts and insist on a dedicated skip. Consider the quants involved, as this could be the only time that a mini-skip could be cost effective. None will allow you to include any asbestos-related materials in a non-dedicated container, and this means anything that remotely looks like it may have asbestos in it. I have known circumstances where a waste carrier has brought the full skip back to site for a few bits of cement fibre roof sheeting to be removed, which involved the skip being totally emptied then re-filled without the offending pieces.

Some local authority transfer stations (local tip) will allow domestic users to take relatively small amounts of asbestos-related products to them for disposal free of charge.

Otherwise, the larger skip companies will provide a dedicated skip (at a cost), but there are a few hoops to jump through to register the site with Department of Environment (DOE), which I will cover elsewhere.

**In a new build**, a lot of the above will not apply unless demolishing, in which case Demo Co will organise, and from that point, you should have a relatively clear site. The groundworks contractor will take care, one way or the other, of the inert material within his package.

However, during the course of the build, you will still have mixed waste to remove, and with it, the same issues of where to store it.

# 19

# Building Warranty

Building warranty, or to use its correct term, Buildings Structural Defects Warranty, is in effect an insurance policy put in place to protect the policy holder, who could be someone else if you sell the property at a later stage, but who will demonstrate compliance with correct construction methods. Like all other insurances, this type of insurance is based on managing risk.

Although some insurers provide a product for refurb and conversion works, in the main, it is aimed at the new build. To warranty a conversion or refurb is a different kettle of fish for all concerned, with significantly more hoops to jump through - therefore, more expensive for all concerned. With that in mind, this chapter is aimed at the new build constructor.

The usual term of a warranty is 10 years, although I am aware of one company that will allow you to extend the period to 12 years.

Think of it as another layer of building control, where as long as you are constructing correctly to the design and the detailing, it is a relatively simple process to achieve – if you know what you are doing.

NHBC is the generic name for warranty providers – in the same way that hoover is for a vacuum cleaner – and up until about 10 years ago held the market in Zurich for providing structural warranty. Indeed, it was always referred to as NHBC cover. As a building main contractor, I was a Zurich-resisted builder with A1 status for 15 years, simply because I preferred working with them and appreciated their procedures towards the builder. Since I constructed most of my builds in one geographic area, I could build a relationship with the area surveyor on the basis of mutual respect for a high quality build.

Clearly, Zurich saw the writing on the wall and decided to withdraw from this side of their business at the same time as the concept of self-building exploded, bringing with it many other companies offering warranties.

Now there are some self-builders out there who are tempted to forego this ingredient of their build, and in my mind, this is at best unwise and at least a false economy.

Since the policy lasts for 10 years, you may think that your plans to live in your dream home for many more years than that will negate the need, and so, save you £2000 – £3000 on average.

Let me give you an illustration that could make you reconsider your decision. I had an email a short while ago from a lady in Cornwall, seeking my advice on the trouble she was having selling her house, which she and her husband and had self-built 2 years previously. She had tracked me down via my website and contacted me because of my significant knowledge and experience of timber frame construction.

The house was timber frame, built for them to live in forever, but personal circumstances had suddenly changed; and so, the house had to be sold.

The enquiry initially came as she was having problems with the sale – a surveyor had convinced her that since it was timber frame with a certain detail, which I will explore in a chapter on timber frame construction, the potential buyer was having trouble raising a mortgage. Whilst exploring this detail with her, I asked if there was a building warranty in place (which would have highlighted the potential issue with the detail at the build stage), you can guess the answer. Their decision at the time was based on the feeling that they would live there forever. They did not really understand the nuts and bolts of the need for a warranty, and there were better uses for the two or three grand at the time. It came to pass that the absence of a warranty was the actual reason for the difficulty, as the issue with the detail could be solved with straightforward mechanics.

I pointed her towards a company that supplied retrospective warranties; but this of course, lost the sale at the time and cost significantly more than the money saved in the first place.

In my opinion, a warranty should be included in the costing as a commodity in the same way as the plumbing or plastering. You do, of course, have the choice technically, as you will not be breaking any laws or sidestepping legislation if you choose not to include it. But it is a brave man (or woman), dare I say foolish, who does not insure themselves in this way.

The reality is that if you are turning to a lender to fund your build, it is pretty well obligatory to put a warranty in place.

Likewise, when someone goes to buy your house at some stage, their lender will insist on a warranty being in place if the house is under 10 years old.

Each of the above are also in the business of managing risk!

So, assuming that you are going to buy a warranty, let's explore the mechanics.

At the time of writing this book, in my mind there are two companies out there that provide a good, user-friendly policy: LABC and Buildzone. I have to emphasise that I have no agenda or affinity to either, as I am currently working with both for different clients.

LABC - although technically have nothing to do with Local Authority Building Control - quite confusingly, share the same logo and have an unusual partnership with the latter, which can sometimes be helpful.

By and large, LABC employ their own in-house surveyors who are allocated a set geographical area to work in. It is, therefore, more than likely that if your friend was building in the same town using LABC warranty, you would be dealing with the same surveyor.

Buildzone, on the other hand, whilst providing a similar product, outsource their surveying to a set of architects/building surveyors, which, in my opinion, does not always work. I recently had a build in Windsor (Berkshire) where the client had chosen Buildzone, and the surveyor was based in Swansea South Wales). Whilst technically this worked very well, logistically it did not.

The criteria for LABC and Buildzone is slightly different, but the end product to the best of my knowledge is equally respected.

Numerous companies out there now offer warranties, Premier being one, but they are actually LABC Warranty quite bizarrely working under a different name. NHBC are still out there as the front runners - especially with the larger house builders - and are heavily involved in many other aspects of the industry.

However, I have an opinion (surprise surprise!) on their suitability and practicality as user-friendly suppliers for the self-builder, which is probably best kept to myself in print. Nevertheless, do not be influenced by my opinion. The important aspect of this chapter is to explain what a warranty does and its importance to have one, not for me to voice who may or may not be the better choice.

All of the above will offer private building control services as opposed to using Local Authority Building Control (confusingly, the real LABC), but that is the subject of a different chapter.

On the subject of which warranty to choose, some lenders will favour certain providers; so if you are borrowing for your build, a bit of investigation on this front would be worth it before you decide. Likewise, it appears that geography sometimes plays a part in choosing the warranty provider, so again a bit of research could pay dividends. As I said earlier, this product is about managing risk.

So on to the mechanics.

Assuming you have had your quote(s), made your decision, and coughed up the premium. You will then be assigned a dedicated surveyor and the technical audit trail will be triggered.

Initially, this will mean the surveyor will begin gathering information in the form of detailed drawings, structural details, ground surveys, and a whole host of factual documents for him to pore over with a view to comforting himself that all ducks are in a row. This information is quite often a movable feast with certain elements still in design, which would fall in to place as the works proceed.

Part of the technical audit involves strategic site inspections, so in effect, the surveyor can satisfy himself that you are building what is designed and agreed upon, correctly.

I mentioned earlier that you should consider this another layer of building control and welcome the surveyor's input. Quite naturally, if you are literally managing the build yourself without the aid of a professional such as myself, you can expect a certain higher level of interest from the surveyor for him to satisfy himself and the insurer that you are building correctly and knowledgeably, therefore ... you guessed it – managing their risk.

My advice would be to exploit the significant knowledge and experience that this person carries and can bring to the table, but do not consider him (or her) as the monster to be placated. Don't forget, he is on your side and you can bet that whatever you are building, he has some form of experience. In the case of some form of revolutionary modern method of construction (MMC), he will help you with difficult detailing. Bear in mind here that it is not part of his brief to help you design in the same way it is not for Building Control, but my experience with all surveyors I have encountered is that they are more than happy to scratch their heads with you and explore ways forward.

Each time you reach the agreed strategic point for their inspection, the surveyor will need to be called to site.

Each different company have different criteria for notice periods to organise the site visit, which may also be a point for you to consider when you are deciding whom to go with. If managing the build yourself, this is a valuable time and one that you would be wise to involve yourself in. In the event that the surveyor sees something that he feels is not correct or needs addressing, you can then explore both this and the future stage one on one.

A written notice will then be produced from the inspection and sent to you, which will describe any outstanding audit documents and any 'defects' found at the inspection requiring remedial action.

What this may be will dictate what happens next, but it will be carefully documented as part of the audit, which then forms part of the file for the eventual final inspection.

When you do reach the final inspection, the surveyor will require similar (but not necessary all) certification that Building Control do that can only have been produced at the completion stage, such as elect sign-off, Part P certificate, or the as-built SAP showing the air leakage test result.

Once all outstanding items are satisfied, the completion certificate is created, and the second stage of the policy kicks in. You then have your buildings structural defects warranty in place and that box is ticked.

# 20

# Going Out to Tender

So, you have your schedule of works and your detailed drawings, structural engineer's designs, surveys, and so on. The next thing is to establish just how much the project is going to cost and to find the people to do it.

It is now time to go out to tender and obtain quotes.

There are basically three ways of going about this: first, get a quantity surveyor (QS) to create a bill of quantities (BoQ); second, to send out drawings and SoW to different trades and ask for a quotation; and third, a combination of the two which is my preferred method.

On the basis that a quotation from a trade is only as good as the information that you have given him (or her), let's explore the three options;

## Get a QS to create a Bill of Quants

A bill of quantities is a document created by a QS that involves firstly measuring or 'taking off' the numerous individual items as specified in the schedule of works and drawings.

This is either shown in a unit form as a square metre ($M^2$), cubic metre ($M^3$), linear metre (M), or number (no). During the course of his measurement, for the sake of calculation, he will, if asked, factor in any wastage on items that will be specified in the document, or if not measured 'net' for contractors to decide their own wastage. He will then apply standard method of measure (SMM) to each item, which will in turn differ according to geography and any other deciding factors. Whilst in most cases materials are much the same cost throughout the country, labour rates in, say, Newcastle are significantly different from London, which are then reflected in the rate to give a true figure.

At some points, there will quite possibly be the need for provisional (prov) or prime cost (pc) sums for, say, the cost of the undecided kitchen or sanitary ware, but these would be itemised and shown accordingly.

Likewise, it will be decided whether or not to incorporate any profits and overheads (P&O), which, of course, will be included by most trades to some degree according to the size of their individual organisation. Having said that, my experience is that to indicate at cost is a reasonable benchmark, since many subbies do not apply SMMs to their costing. A view needs to be taken, which again, unfortunately, can be a post code lottery.

According to how the SoW is broken down, the unit rate will include all aspects in that item – for example, (broadly) with the brickwork, it will include not only the bricks, but the sand and cement, the sundry items such as wall ties, the mixer and the cost of running it, the labour to mix the mortar and load the bricks, and of course, the labour cost of the bricklayer.

These calculations will show in a separate column with the figures – xxx $m^2$ @ £yy.z = £Abc.dd.

This will apply to each and every item and arrive at a total cost. I have shown an example below.

**2.3 - Construction of the New Building**

**2.3.6 - External Face Brickwork**

| Ref | Description | Quantity | Units | Rate | Value |
|---|---|---|---|---|---|
| | **BRICKWORK** | | | | |
| | Face Brickwork, bucket handle pointed; PC £550 per 1000 in cement mortar (1:3) | | | | |
| | Walls below DPC: | | | | |
| A | 102.5 mm | 12 | m2 | 65.18 | 782.16 |
| | Polyethylene damp proof course; 100 mm laps sealed with adhesive tape; in cement mortar (1:3) pointing where exposed | | | | |
| B | 100 mm wide | 52 | m | 2.11 | 109.72 |
| | Face Brickwork, bucket handle pointed; PC £550 per 1000 in cement mortar (1:3) | | | | |
| | Walls above DPC: | | | | |
| C | 102.5 mm | 247 | m2 | 65.18 | 16,099.46 |
| | Chimney | | | | |
| | Projections of chimney breasts in: | | | | |
| D | stretcher bond | 17 | m2 | 84.71 | 1,440.07 |
| | Blocks, face size 440 x 215 mm; in gauged mortar (1:2:9) | | | | |
| | Inner leaf of chimney; | | | | |
| E | 100 mm | 5 | m2 | 46.33 | 231.65 |
| | Flue linings; | | | | |
| F | Flue linings 185 mm internal diameter | 7 | m | 47.26 | 330.82 |
| G | Extra for: bend | 2 | Nr | 37.45 | 74.90 |
| | Chimney pots; setting and flaunching in cement mortar (1:3) | | | | |
| | Tapered roll top chimney pot: | | | | |
| | | | | To Collection: | 19,068.78 |

**2.3-2.3.6/1**

The creation of a BoQ should cost £300-£500, but in my mind, it is an investment.

**Send out the SoW to the trades and ask for quotations**
Part of the information that you will need to give the relevant trades will include exactly what they should be quoting for and including. The object here is to ensure like-for-like quotes, and also, that all items throughout the SoW are covered. You want to arrive at a cost conclusion that leaves no stone unturned or nasty surprises later.

You should send the SoW in its entirety so the contractor gets a complete picture of the works, and you should always list the reference number of each item to be quoted, insisting that each item be quoted separately. The importance of this is that should any item be omitted or changed, it should be easy to know what figure needs adjusting or omitting. The individual figures would later be used with the successful contractor to structure a payment valuation. I will cover the mechanics of this in a later chapter. The contractor will then do his own take off (measuring), but in most cases, you would not know how many units of each item he has based his calculations on, nor the rate that he has used. He would quote each item including any mark up as definitive sums. If VAT is to be charged, this should be separated at this stage to avoid confusion. It is always best to deal with net figures. To be fair, different trades have different ways of pricing according to the trade itself and the experience of the person quoting. You then have the element of how badly he wants the job, which will of course, dictate the rates applied.

## Combination of the two

Whilst the BoQ gives you a good indication of the costing, it also provides useful information to you and the trades who are quoting. If you are able to confirm to the roofing contractor exactly how many M2 of tiles he would need or how many Ml of valley, you help him make sure that the quote is accurate. Believe me, a contractor such as a roofer is far more likely to have tiles left over than not enough, since he will err on the side of caution when doing his own take off.

Once again, the more information that you can provide, the more likelihood of accurate like-for-like quotations, and no matter how good the SoW, the inclusion of information in the BoQ will add to the picture.

To clarify here, the QS will provide you with a copy of the BoQ without rates, to send out. The information on the cost version is just for you. To this extent, in theory, the only difference between two quotes should be the amount of P&O, if any, that the different contractors expect to make.

## Choosing the Contractors to Go Out To

Many contractors will provide elaborate costing and quantities that have been created on pricing software. Impressive and informative as it may appear, in reality, this is not of any significant value at this stage, and so, you should return it to him asking for the items as shown in the SoW to be priced individually. Whilst a take-off style of pricing is useful for showing that certain materials have been quantified correctly, the document would be more for his use rather than your own. Only when you are ready to talk turkey with him would you be wanting to interrogate perhaps how he has arrived at the figure for each element. The important thing at this stage is for him to supply numbers in a format that can easily be compared, and that is the reason for your request.

This discipline firstly enables you to see where a contractor might be strong or weak with his figures when comparing with others. It also then forms part of the agreement when awarding the works so it is very straightforward to establish a value when calculating what should or should not be paid at valuation stages.

Two things are very important here: first, that all items are covered somewhere by a contractor; but second so like-for-like quotes are received for you to compare.

The object of the exercise is to arrive at an eventual final figure knowing that ALL works are included and the figure is accurate.

Do not be seduced by the cheapest quote. I will cover this when investigating the individual aspects and their quotations later.

For eventual draw-down purposes, I would usually create a spreadsheet for each element, breaking it down into the item numbers with figures, so a percentage can be drawn against the item and the remainder carried on to the next valuation.

The other advantage of such a discipline is that should an item be omitted, then it is straightforward to deduct the figure with no ambiguity.

By far, the best way to find the right contractor is by word of mouth; other than that you will be Googling or using the local directory.

It is important, however, to make sure that you are approaching the right size (and I don't mean how heavy he is) contractor.

The carpenter who made a brilliant job of your neighbour's fitted wardrobes is unlikely to be geared up or interested in the first and second fix carpentry works on a new build house. Domestic tradesmen have a totally different mind-set and discipline towards subbies who work on larger construction projects, and will rarely be competitive in price. This will make your task to find the right one harder, as there are usually many more of the former than the latter; but persevere – the right man for the right job is of paramount importance.

Beware also of the crossover tradesman. You want a carpenter for carpentry works and a plumber for plumbing. The man who claims to be able to offer both is a dead giveaway to me regarding the level of work that he is used to working on.

A dedicated trade will be more professional, responsible, and cost effective.

On the subject of responsibility, apart from a few key items, I firmly believe that the most efficient way is to box off the trades and have them quote on a supply-and-fix basis. Apart from the VAT element on a new build that I will cover in a different chapter (supply-and-fix carries a zero VAT implication, whereas on supply only you will be paying the VAT and then entering into a VAT reclaim scheme at the end of the works), there is the very important aspect of areas of responsibility. You may think that you will save some money if you supply the materials and the contractor works on a labour-only basis. But apart from speaking volumes regarding the size and capability of the contractor, it will be your problem when a delivery turns up with a shortage to follow, or a damaged item, and when the contractor then charges extra for lost time or a return visit. Consider also the scenario where the carpenter has run out of screws (he will not tell you until he is using the last one!) and will then be kicking his heels till you run down the builder's merchant to pick up a box.

The best one is where the bricky's labourer tells you he needs more cement as he is opening up the last bag, or where (I could waffle on and on regarding this subject with enough to write a book of its own) you have organised a delivery for Tuesday, knowing that the tradesman is due on Wednesday, the delivery does not turn up but the tradesman does; he cannot do anything so charges you for a wasted journey and cannot get back for a week. In the majority of cases where a contractor is used to supply and fix, no matter what deal you think you have created with the merchant, and that includes the promises given with delivery schedules, the subbie has better buying power than you, so much so that he will include it within his quote and still make his margin.

One last point on this subject (I promise) is that if the plumber supplied the WC pan and it leaks at the joint, it is his problem with no wiggle room for 'I didn't supply it so it's not my issue'. Also, how can he register and guarantee the boiler if he did not supply it? There is nothing wrong, when the time comes, for you to specify and negotiate the price of the sanitary ware, even from a particular bathroom shop, but have him purchase it and take responsibility. Sure he will want to include an amount for his trouble (and ownership) but this is a small price to pay for your peace of mind.

You have probably gathered by now, dear reader, that I do not subscribe to this stressful and inefficient way forward.

In an ideal world, you need three quotes back for each element. Do not underestimate how long this will take and plan ahead accordingly. I find on average that in order to get three quotes back, you will send out to five, and although I am generalising - as some trades (MVHR or perhaps Solar Pv) will respond a lot better than others - be prepared for contractors indicating their enthusiasm at initial contact stage but never returning the quote.

On that note, do not simply fire off bundles to unknown contractors without speaking to them first and getting a feel of their capabilities, no matter how elaborate their website. It is guaranteed to waste your time.

With patience and effort, you should arrive at a list of quotes back that will then help confirm the costs and select the correct contractors.

To conclude this chapter, the process above will prove to be very challenging, especially for the first timer, and you will need plenty of patience and time. So don't leave it for too late or give up until you have more than one quote in for every element.

In the next chapter, I would like to share with you an abridged version of an article that I wrote a little while ago regarding finding good quality contractors and subbies at the right price. Perhaps it will help you in your quest for the right ones.

# 21

# What Happened to all the Good Tradesmen?

Since a great deal of my time involves finding and vetting tradesmen on behalf of my clients, it goes without saying that the dwindling numbers of quality craftsmen (and sometimes craftswomen) are of concern to me.

Many formally trained and qualified people are reaching a certain age and, therefore, looking towards throttling back. However, they are not, unfortunately, being replaced at the same rate as their decline. Whilst there are still many, good quality, motivated and genuine tradesmen out there, the ratio between good and not so good has taken a downward shift over the past 20 years and is showing no signs of improving any time soon.

One of the major reasons for the decline is that youngsters leaving school do not have the same motivation towards any form of manual work.

I left school at 15, and by the age of 16, was embroiled in the construction industry. It was instilled in me to learn a trade for the good of my future; I was brought up to recognise the value of hard work, and so, the building industry was considered the way forward. I had a thirst for knowledge that took me through a five-year carpentry apprenticeship followed by numerous management and surveying qualifications. That same thirst still carries me on today, following the invention of modern methods of construction, sustainability, and energy performance. Sadly today, that attitude is rare, with a construction future being the last resort rather than the first. Couple that with the average 16 year old's attention span lasting the length of a short computer game. And what chance do we have of recruiting someone who needs to invest several years before he can boast of being a tradesman? The 16 year old wants to be a chippy after 5 weeks, not 5 years, and earn the big bucks. Also, what about the embarrassment of mum dropping him off at work the same as she has for the past 12 years!

16 year olds are seduced (and more than a little pressured by mum and dad) into 'further education', which is mainly a numbers game for governments and universities. How often do we hear of university graduates being unable to find a job at 23 because the three-year BA degree in underwater basket weaving proved to be not so useful as advertised. If a young lad leaves school at 16 nowadays, he is considered uneducated and borderline useless.

Another perpetrator of the dwindling number of high quality trained tradesmen is the unhealthy attitude of the client. For most small and medium-sized jobs, the main criteria is cost rather than quality.

This thinking breeds the introduction of 'trades' whose training took the form of a job seeker's six-week course and so will work for less than the man who formally trained for 5 years. One thing is for sure: if you are getting the works done cheap, then you are getting a cheap job. Can you really expect quality when you continually haggle on the price?

The enormous influx of low-earning European workers over the past decade is mainly down to the perpetual want for the employer to get the job done cheap. Whilst arguably there are many seasoned tradesmen from Europe, my experience is that whilst they provide the enthusiasm and hard work ethic, the majority sadly lack in the understanding of our construction methods and regulations, making them a difficult entity unsupervised. You don't have to be Einsteinski to work out the probability of the works being completed on time, technically correct, and to a high quality, but until our tradesmen are shown the respect for their training reflected in the amount they are paid, then the whole topic will continue spinning on its axis.

Of course, there are many building workers who not only charge a lot but provide an inferior job, and that's where my role comes into play. There are still, thankfully, a number of well-informed, formally trained craftsmen out there, and when I bring a team of such to the table, you can be sure that my knowledge and experiences have ensured the best quality for the budget.

However, the job becomes more challenging with the passing of time and tradesmen.

# 22

# Notices

In anticipation of works commencing, you should give notice to a few people / organisations.

Let's assume that you have your planning approval, pre-conditions are sorted, Building Regs are under control, as is building warranty.

If demolishing, you will need to have notified Building Control with:

## A Section 80 Demolition Notice

If you are planning to carry out demolition work greater than 50 $m^3$ in volume (some exemptions apply), you will need to notify the council before you start under Section 80 of the Building Act 1984 (the Act). The controls for demolition work are given under Section 80–83 of the Act, of which the entire written volume is approximately the size of a two-storey residential rear extension.

An application form should be filled out and submitted to the council at least six weeks before the work is due to start. Demolition works should not commence until either the six weeks have elapsed or a notice is served by the council under Section 81 of the Act.

Your notification should include all of the information stipulated in Section 80. Specifically, the following details under Point 3 of the Act are required:

(3) A notice under subsection (2) above shall specify the building to which it relates and the works of demolition intended to be carried out, and it is the duty of a person giving such a notice to a local authority to send or give a copy of it to:

(i) the occupier of any building adjacent to the building,

(ii) any public gas supplier in whose authorised area the building is situated,

(iii) the public electricity supplier in whose authorised area the building is situated and any other person authorised by a licence under that part to supply electricity to the building.

Following receipt of a Section 80 notice, the council will issue a counter notice under Section 81 of the Building Control Act 1984, which will detail various conditions to ensure that the work is carried out safely. Demolition should not commence unless:

(1) the council has given a notice under Section 81; or,
(ii) six weeks have elapsed since the Section 80 notice was made to the council.

Any self-respecting Demo co will insist on sight of evidence to confirm the date of the Section 80 submission if over six weeks, or that of Section 81 if under.

## Notify the Health & Safety Executive

Form F10 Notification of a Construction project

Although all CDM obligations and regulations will be covered in their own chapter, notification of the works commencing must be filed. There is an online procedure for this.

Regulation 6 of the CDM regulations requires that the client must give notice in writing to the HSE as soon as is practicable before the construction phase begins, or arrange for someone else to do this on their behalf.

The notice must include the details included in Schedule 1 of the regulations:

- The date of forwarding the notice.
- The address of the construction site or precise description of its location.
- The name of the local authority where the construction site is located.
- A brief description of the project and the construction work that it entails.
- The following contact details of the client: name, address, telephone number, and (if available) an email address.
- The following contact details of the principal designer: name, address, telephone number, and (if available) an email address.
- The following contact details of the principal contractor: name, address, telephone number, and (if available) an email address.
- The date planned for the start of the construction phase.

- The time allocated by the client under Regulation 4(1) for the construction work.
- The planned duration of the construction phase.
- The estimated maximum number of people at work on the construction site.
- The planned number of contractors on the construction site.
- The name and address of any contractor already appointed.
- The name and address of any designer already appointed.
- A declaration signed by or on behalf of the client that the client is aware of the client duties under these Regulations.

Where details are not available (such as the details of the principal contractor), they must be provided when they are available, and in any event, before construction works begin.

The notice must also be clearly displayed in the construction site office in a comprehensible form where it can be read by any worker engaged in the construction work, and if necessary, be periodically updated.

As of 31 March 2015, forms can no longer be submitted personally and have to be completed online.

# 23

# CDM - Health and Safety requirements

An area quite easily underestimated for the self-builder is the health and safety requirements, which from April 2015, are significantly more important.

Construction (Design and Management) (CDM) is a piece of legislation that aims to reduce accidents during construction projects via good design, planning, and co-operation from concept to completion and, ultimately, decommissioning. It also specifies legal requirements on site safety standards and specifies the need for the provision of welfare facilities such as access to toilets.

The CDM Regulations were introduced by the Health and Safety Executive (HSE) in 2007 as a means of improving health and safety on UK construction sites and reducing the risk of harm to those who have to build, use and maintain structures. They impose legal duties on virtually everybody involved in the construction process, including clients, designers, and contractors, from the inception of a project to final demolition and removal. For the purposes of the CDM regulations, these people are often referred to as 'duty holders'.

The 2007 CDM regulations actually applied to all sites, though this was not widely understood. There were additional duties for 'notifiable' projects –projects that took longer than 30 business days or 500 person days. These included the requirement for the client to appoint a 'CDM coordinator' and 'principal contractor'. The CDM coordinator had the legal responsibility to advise and assist the client on all of its health and safety duties and provide pre-construction information to the contractor. The principal contractor, meanwhile, had to develop a health and safety plan from this information and ensure that it was followed.

On 6 April 2015, a new version of the regulations – CDM 2015 – was introduced. The update was partly prompted by suggestions that there was still a lack of integration between health and safety requirements and design in the pre-construction phase of projects. It was argued that the CDM co-ordinator was often appointed too late to be embedded effectively in the pre-construction team.

The HSE also felt that instances of unacceptable standards were persisting, particularly on smaller sites. CDM 2015 will, therefore, bring greater focus on smaller projects, as well as place new obligations on clients and facilities managers, through a number of significant changes. These include:

- Extending the scope of the regulations to include domestic clients.
- Removing the role of the CDM coordinator.

- Introducing a new duty holder: the principal designer.
- Appointing a principal designer and principal contractor not only on 'notifiable projects' but on all schemes where two or more contractors are on site (to 'catch' smaller projects).
- Changing the project notification threshold.

It is in the interests of everybody involved in construction projects, but particularly those who procure them, to know and understand these obligations. The following will outline the major changes, and explain what they mean.

## The Client's Role

Under CDM 2007, the CDM coordinator was the client's key safety adviser. The removal of this role, therefore, has a significant impact on project safety governance. If you are a client, you must make suitable arrangements for managing a project, including the allocation of time and other resources. Clients' key responsibilities include:

- Notifying the HSE of the project details and confirming that the project team are aware of their duties.
- Ensuring duty holders comply with their duties.
- Providing the pre-construction information.
- Ensuring that the minimum health and safety standards are maintained on site.
- Ensuring that the construction phase health and safety plan is drawn up by the principal contractor.
- Ensuring that a health and safety file is produced by the principal designer.

Perhaps the client's most important duty is to appoint a principal designer and principal contractor, which are mandatory even on projects with more than one contractor. In practice, these duty holders will carry out many of the functions listed above – although it is still the client's duty to ensure that they are performing their roles. The client must make these two appointments 'as soon as practicable'. In particular, the principal designer should be appointed as early as possible in the design process, ideally at concept stage. This will help the client to pull together the pre-construction information, such as asbestos surveys, existing health and safety files, and structural drawings.

Failure to make these appointments will see the principle designer and principle contractor duties (as outlined in the next sections) transfer automatically to the client.

The exceptions to this part of the regulations is domestic clients, defined in CDM 2015 as 'clients for whom a construction project is carried out which is not done in connection with a business'. On domestic projects, most client duties are passed to other duty holders, and should the client fail to appoint a principal designer and contractor, these roles fall automatically to the designer in control of the pre-construction phase and the contractor in control of the construction phase of the project.

## The Principal Designer's Role

The new role of the principal designer takes on many of the duties of the CDM coordinator, although it is not a direct replacement. The principal designer must plan, manage, monitor, and co-ordinate health and safety in the pre-construction phase of a project. This includes:

- Identifying, eliminating, or controlling foreseeable risks.

- Ensuring designers carry out their duties.
- Preparing and providing relevant information to other duty holders.
- Providing relevant information to the principal contractor to help them plan, manage, monitor, and co-ordinate health and safety in the construction phase.

The principal designer does not need to be the lead designer on the project; it should never be assumed that the lead designer takes on this role by default and the appointment must be made in writing. CDM 2015 includes in its definition of designers: 'architects, architectural technologists, consulting engineers, quantity surveyors, interior designers, temporary works engineers, chartered surveyors, technicians or anyone who specifies or alters a design'. It also states that the principal designer must be 'an organisation or an individual with sufficient knowledge, experience and ability to carry out the role'.

### The Principal Contractor's Role

This remains largely unchanged from CDM 2007. The principal contractor must plan, manage, monitor ,and co-ordinate health and safety in the construction phase of a project. This includes:

- Liaising with the client and principal designer.
- Preparing the construction phase plan.
- Organising co-operation between contractors and co-ordinating their work.
- Ensuring suitable site conditions are provided.

## The Manufacturer's Role

If, say, on a roof refurbishment project where the manufacturer might directly be advising the client on design and specification, it is the duty of the manufacturer to inform the client of its responsibilities under the regulations, and in other scenarios, it will be their duty as a designer to comply with the requests of the principal designer.

## Notification Threshold

Under CDM 2015, the HSE will need to be notified about projects exceeding 500 person days or 'longer than 30 working days' with 'more than 20 workers working simultaneously'.

This should have the effect of reducing the number of notifiable projects.

The easiest way to notify any project to the HSE or other relevant enforcing authority is to use the online notification form F10 on the HSE's website. Further information on how to notify construction work can be found at **www.hse.gov.uk/construction/cdm/faq/notification.htm.**

It is important to note that clients, designers, and contractors still have responsibilities for those projects for which the HSE does not require notification.

## Transitional Arrangements

The HSE recognises that there are construction projects that started before the CDM 2015 regulations came into force and continue beyond that date. For these projects (as long as there is more than one contractor involved), the following transitional arrangements apply.

Where the construction phase has not yet started and the client has not yet appointed a CDM coordinator, the client must appoint a principal designer as soon as practicable.

If the CDM coordinator has already been appointed, the client must appoint a principal designer to replace them by 6 October 2015, unless the project comes to an end before then.

In the period it takes to appoint the principal designer, the appointed CDM coordinator should comply with the duties contained in Schedule 4 of CDM 2015. These reflect the duties placed on CDM coordinators under CDM 2007 rather than requiring them to act as principal designers – a role for which they may not be equipped.

Pre-construction information, construction phase plans, or health and safety files provided under CDM 2007 are

recognised as meeting the equivalent requirements in CDM 2015.

Any project that was notified under CDM 2007 is still recognised as a notification under CDM 2015.

A principal contractor appointed under CDM 2007 will be considered to be a principal contractor under CDM 2015.

Now, for the self-builder using sub-contractors, all of the above is not necessarily easy to negotiate and categorise, as opposed to a client employing a main contractor.

What I will say, though, is that ignorance is no excuse if something goes wrong, and all the documentation and legislation in the world cannot compensate for knowledge and common sense.

Whilst the regulations focus on roles and statutory requirements, my opinion is that anyone embarking on a half decent-sized project would benefit from a basic health and safety awareness course that most site workers have to have completed just to be allowed on site. Such a course for £150 - £200 would teach you the 'how to' bit to complement the 'who should'.

# 24

# Costing, Programme, and Cashflow

While there may be no such thing as a 'typical' self-build project - each coming with its unique set of challenges and opportunities - every project does have identifiable stages of development, from the initial digging of the foundations to the final fix.

If borrowing for the build, as the value of the constructed work increases, your lender will release a percentage of your overall funds, so it is critical that you understand exactly what your project is going to cost you at each stage to meet your expenses. Even if you are self-funding, you will still need information as to when monies will be required.

A programme of the works, in whatever form, then helps create the picture for the funds to be available, so effectively, the two are the same.

Make sure that you've worked out precisely how much money you'll need to pay out for materials, tradesmen, and specialist services at each stage so that your available funds match your project. For example, a timber construction is more expensive in the early stages than a brick and block build, as you have to pay for the whole system upfront. It's also essential to have agreed payment terms with builders and other tradespeople in advance of work starting. If you don't have a good handle on your cash flow – that is, if you haven't matched your finances to your projected expenses at each stage – then you might find that you're unable to meet your contractors' invoices or pay for the materials you need. Either situation can hinder progress or, in the worst case scenario, your contractor may leave your project and move on to another job if they haven't been paid, or don't have materials to work with.

For many people, the whole point of self-building is to make the money they have available for a home go further – so it follows that accurately planning and managing a budget should be a primary concern. This process should start well before you even buy your plot of land, and shouldn't finish until you've paid the final contractor and jumped though all the hoops to reclaim VAT on your building materials.

When you first begin to work out your budget, it makes sense to plan out and weigh up the costs of all the different aspects of your project – even if that means working in round numbers. You should have a total figure in mind that you want to work towards – whether you are borrowing money or not – and a simple pie chart is a good ready reckoner to start with.

For the self-builder or renovator, getting the budget right has always been important. But in these post credit crunch times, it's absolutely critical.

Once you've got the basic figures in place, you'll then need to spend significant amounts of time planning everything down to the smallest detail – because today, it is more difficult than ever to negotiate extra lending if you overspend in the early stages of the build.

## Costing

Let's assume that you have received all of your quotes back, and you are reaching conclusions on who is doing what; so, you need to create a tool for how much it will cost you.

Whilst there are literally dozens of project management tools out there of varying complexity, to my mind, the simplest are often the best, and when it comes to a costing sheet for the works, a basic spreadsheet works, as it is straightforward to adjust and can evolve to form a payment record as shown in this chapter.

I have shown a very basic spreadsheet, but as you can see, it gives as little or as much information as you might want to incorporate. Down the side is the list of elements, with the agreed cost added in the next column. Just to show indicative columns, I have included additional works, but quite simply, you can add or omit whatever information you (or say a lender) may require.

The important aspect is that you have a simple, workable method of integrating information, and it can be combined with the program to create the cashflow forecast.

| Draw down record | | | | | |
|---|---|---|---|---|---|
| Trade | Amount Net | Additional works | Contractor | Draw 1 May | Remaining |
| Set up site/welfare/temp protect | | | | | |
| Groundworks inc drainage to DPC | £43,092.00 | | J Blogs | £18,320.00 | £24,772.00 |
| Block shell | £9,932.00 | | an other | | £9,932.00 |
| Timber Frame | £20,800.64 | -£100.00 | J Blogs | £16,000.00 | £4,700.64 |
| Scaffolding | £3,500.00 | | an other | | £3,500.00 |
| Roof coverings | £9,860.00 | | J Blogs | | £9,860.00 |
| Carpentry Works inc fascias & Windows | £25,164.00 | | an other | | £25,164.00 |
| Plastering inc associate works/floor screed | £13,651.72 | £215.52 | J Blogs | | £13,867.24 |
| Plumbing/heating | £16,400.00 | | an other | | £16,400.00 |
| Elect instalation | £7,641.00 | | J Blogs | | £7,641.00 |
| MVHR | £4,443.00 | | an other | | £4,443.00 |
| Kitchen install | | | J Blogs | | £0.00 |
| Finishings (tiling etc) | | | an other | | £0.00 |
| General attendance | | | J Blogs | | £0.00 |
| Decorate | £4,220.00 | | an other | | £4,220.00 |
| Mastic | £250.00 | | J Blogs | | £250.00 |
| Floor coverings | | | an other | | £0.00 |
| | ########## | | | | |
| Fees | | | | | |
| Management | | | | | |
| Engineer | | | | | |
| Building Control | | | | | |
| Architect | | | | | |
| Building Warranty | | | | | |
| Contingencies | | | | | |
| | | | Total draw | £34,320.00 | |
| | ########## | | | | £124,749.88 |

## Programme of Works

When it comes to a creating a programme for the works, a simply created spreadsheet works, as with the spreadsheet it is straightforward to adjust.

Basically, the tasks to be completed are identified and listed down the left-hand column and blocks of time are shaded in the corresponding row to show the start date, finish date, and the duration of each task. Additional columns can be added for budget costs, actual costs, and the resources required for each task. It can be as detailed and complex as you wish to make it.

The example that follows shows a simple pie chart with the tasks broken down into individual trades. For a project management tool such as this to work effectively, it needs to be completed as accurately as possible at the earliest time. To do this, you need to gather as much information as possible. If items are missed or an unrealistic schedule is set, the project will be destined for problems before it even gets underway.

Program of Works

| | 13-Jul | 20-Jul | 27-Jul | 03-Aug | 10-Aug | 17-Aug | 24-Aug | 31-Aug | 07-Sep | 14-Sep | 21-Sep | 28-Sep | 05-Oct | 12-Oct | 19-Oct | 26-Oct |
|---|---|---|---|---|---|---|---|---|---|---|---|---|---|---|---|---|
| Weeks | 1 | 2 | 3 | 4 | 5 | 6 | 7 | 8 | 9 | 10 | 11 | 12 | 13 | 14 | 15 | 16 |
| **Works** | | | | | | | | | | | | | | | | |
| Set up site | | | | | | | | | | | | | | | | |
| Demolition & Removals | | | | | | | | | | | | | | | | |
| Foundations | | | | | | | | | | | | | | | | |
| Drainage | | | | | | | | | | | | | | | | |
| Timber Frame inc structural slab | | | | | | | | | | | | | | | | |
| Scaffolding | | | | | | | | | | | | | | | | |
| Pitched Roof Coverings | | | | | | | | | | | | | | | | |
| Rainwater goods | | | | | | | | | | | | | | | | |
| Flat roof Coverings | | | | | | | | | | | | | | | | |
| Windows install | | | | | | | | | | | | | | | | |
| Brickwork | | | | | | | | | | | | | | | | |
| Carp 1st Fix | | | | | | | | | | | | | | | | |
| Elect 1st fix | | | | | | | | | | | | | | | | |
| Plumbing/heating 1st fix | | | | | | | | | | | | | | | | |
| MVHR | | | | | | | | | | | | | | | | |
| Plastering works | | | | | | | | | | | | | | | | |
| Carp 2nd fix | | | | | | | | | | | | | | | | |
| Elect 2nd fix | | | | | | | | | | | | | | | | |
| Plumbing 2nd Fix | | | | | | | | | | | | | | | | |
| Decorate | | | | | | | | | | | | | | | | |
| Incoming Services | | | | | | | | | | | | | | | | |
| Floor & wall tiling | | | | | | | | | | | | | | | | |
| Internal Finishings | | | | | | | | | | | | | | | | |
| Floor coverings | | | | | | | | | | | | | | | | |
| Ext works | | | | | | | | | | | | | | | | |
| Slippage | | | | | | | | | | | | | | | | |
| Completion | | | | | | | | | | | | | | | | |

## What needs doing?

First off, identify all the tasks that need to be done to complete the build using the task list on the left.

**How long will each task take?**
If you are familiar with house building, then you may be able to enter durations for your tasks from past experience. If not, you will need to get researching again, but the most accurate estimates will be obtained from the people who are doing the work week in, week out. Show prospective tradesmen your plans when you first meet and ask them to give you an idea of timescales along with their estimates. Back it up with your own research.

**Using it to manage your project?**
An accurate programme represented in this way allows you to track when tasks need to occur and organise tradesmen, equipment, and materials accordingly.

If you are procuring materials for your build, be aware of special items such as beam and block floors and roof trusses, which could have lengthy manufacturing lead times. This needs to be accounted for so that they arrive on-site at the right time. Use your chart to identify when they are required and when you need to place an order. You could even add a block to the chart as an order reminder.

The preceding chart clearly displays what should be happening on your project at any point in time. Comparing what is happening on-site to the chart allows you to identify progress.

If the project has slipped, there may be areas in the schedule that can be adjusted to pull it back later on.

# 25

# Contractor Selection and Preparing to Start Works

So, you have received quotes and are faced with the task of selecting the right contractors. Until you have gone a little deeper, the bottom line numbers are not so important, so don't get too excited by what appears to be a good price.

It may seem obvious, but the first thing is to make sure that they are like for like insomuch as that all items as specified have been included. I can guarantee that even though you asked for the quotes to be priced per item, some will have been returned as a lump sum, which no matter what the figure, is of no use to you. You are not asking for a breakdown of how he arrived at the sums, but simply breaking it down item by item for the reasons in the earlier chapter, with each item including any profits or Prime Cost (PC) sums but no VAT if applicable.

Second, create a simple spreadsheet for each trade with the items down one side and the contractors across the top. Now this may seem like a time-consuming job, but it is certainly worth the effort. You then have the straightforward task of filling in the boxes and, therefore, making the comparison and selection process far simpler.

This will show not only if any numbers are missing but also any radically different numbers that highlight that the person quoting has misunderstood the item.

You could then go back to them and confirm.

As I said in a previous chapter, if priced correctly, the figures should all have a pattern, so if all of Contractor A's figures are, say, 10% higher than B, then it is simply a more expensive quote. However, if B and C are similar – apart from one or two items on B that are significantly different – a little checking needs to be done to make sure that the item is understood and priced correctly.

To create a spreadsheet for maybe eight or ten trades could appear arduous, but it has to be right.

When you are satisfied that all quotes have included what they should do, then it's time to make some conclusions.

My first word of warning is do not automatically be seduced by the cheapest quote, and whilst the maxim of 'you get what you pay for' is not always right, more often than not, it is.

If, for example, Quote A is significantly cheaper than B or C, but B and C are in the same ballpark, then the assumption that A is your man may not be the best choice.

Now, subject to which trade we are talking about, the cheaper price could have a different, less obvious significance.

The distinctly cheaper roofing contractor, where you have specified the tile, fittings, and most other items could, therefore, be cheaper than the others for no suspicious reason. He just feels he can do the work quicker and can perhaps buy the tiles cheaper than the others, and so should be seriously considered. In other words, his job is a very straightforward trade with very little room for any potential corner-cutting that could cause tears. The important question is, can he do the job when you agree within the time you agree in a professional manner?

On the other hand if Plumber A is significantly cheaper than B and C, there are a lot of elements left to his design where corners could be cut, for example, with cheap pipe fittings or small time-cutting exercises like not clipping pipes or using cheaper radiators valves.

Having said all of the above, the only way to know is by further investigation.

It is far easier for me to straightforwardly evaluate the selection process above because I have been doing this for a very long time, can read between the lines, know exactly what questions to ask, and so, can work on gut instinct. Your lack of this knowledge is why a recommended contractor can get you part the way there.

If you are converting or re-furbing, then whether or not the contractor is VAT registered could also make a difference to be considered.

A quick note on the apparent worth of a contractor that you do not know. It is a fairly simple task to have an elaborate website with alleged testimonials. Conversely, just because a subbie does not feel the need for a website because he is always busy, or on the odd occasion does not even communicate by email, it does not mean that he would not provide a decent job at the right price delivered on time.

I realise that I am raising more questions than answers here, but by keeping my favourite phrase 'you don't know what you don't know' firmly in mind, hopefully, you will be aware of what to investigate further. Probably, the best way to help you get a feeling for a contractor is to meet him to discuss your job and others that he is working on.

Now I can boast that I have probably come into contact with just about every size, shape, colour, and personality there can possibly be on this planet (not sure that they all were actually human) in this fickle industry, and I can confirm that to stereotype your average construction worker is a fool's errand. Most decent construction workers have a thirst for banter, clearly are prone to the odd profanity, and can bitch like old washer women.

However, in the main, they are friendly, quick-witted, and eager to get the job done and get paid. In my entire 40 odd years, I have only ever seen one punch-up on site; although by listening to them, you would swear that one is just about to erupt every hour.

I have worked with extremely good tradesmen who looked like they were homeless and had not slept for a week. Likewise, I have come across some very slick-looking and –talking people who, upon further discussion, confirmed to me that I would not trust them to build a garden shed the right way up. If a carpenter has arms full of tattoos, do not assume that he will do a bad job, run off with your daughter, or threaten you for extra money. Again, it is easy for me to say; I have employed many of construction's waifs and strays and can spot a good craftsman at 50 paces.

However, if you are prepared to dig a little deeper, you will realise that just because the bricky has green hair and a wooden leg, it does not mean that he cannot lay bricks straight and true and keep to the programme. (Maybe an exaggeration about the wooden leg, but you get my drift).

You will be surprised as to just how many reliable subbies would give you their last rolo in return for your payment on time.

One rule of thumb that I tend to go with is the subbie's vehicle(s), tools, and plant. A good carpenter will have a van full of well-used tools, carefully laid out and protected by a Rottweiler. They are his pride and joy and proof of a disciplined attitude to work and providing a good job. Likewise, the groundworks contractor that owns his own machines (for example, diggers) will impress me more than the one who hires in, and turns up in a pimped up pick-up. They can all talk the talk to the uninitiated, but it's all about filtering through it and forming a relationship.

A fairly important ingredient that I should mention is my 'Swings and Roundabouts' theory. You are embarking on a working relationship with each of these contractors, and the relationship itself is every bit as important as the works that will be provided. The relationship has to be built on a sense of fair play in both directions, and whilst you have the agreed scope of works, believe me, you will not have thought of absolutely everything. It has never happened to me in over 4 decades.

Therefore, part of the selection process will be for you to feel comfortable that the chosen contractor will not be screaming 'extras' every time a slight deviation or very small addition is requested.

Bear in mind though, that this concept works both ways, so a view needs to be taken throughout his entire works when omissions / additions / changes are made. The keyword here is relationship, so there will be a limit as to how far you can push the equation.

Having said all of the above, your experienced contractor – if he has any sense – will have built in small 'buggeration' buffers, especially when dealing with Mr and Mrs Self-Build (no offence intended).

More questions than answers? We are getting there.

If you are seriously going it alone, without a professional to help you with this aspect, then you are undoubtedly dealing with the most important aspect of your entire project. Having said that, there is immense value in getting to know the contractors before works commence, so keep reading.

Now let's assume that you are feeling good about the bricky with the wooden leg. His price sounds right, he understands the job and its involvement, he has another bricky and labourer working with him, an account with local merchants, he drives a half-decent van (it's an automatic and it's his left leg that's wooden), he has plenty of references, is busy, you have been round his house for Sunday lunch and met his grandmother, and you know that he is the right man for the job. So let's look into how you go about agreeing upon his employment.

You have his quote, which effectively forms the first part of a contract between you. Since you are employing him on a sub-contract basis, it is unlikely that you will put a formally prepared contract in place with him. Whilst there are JCT contracts for sub-contractors, they are tedious and not really aimed for works at the level of, say, the build of one house.

The majority of other formal contracts – JCT contract for intermediate works, for example – are designed for main contractor employment, so do not apply to the self-builder employing sub-contractors.

In which case, you create your own contract!

Now in reality, a contract is an agreement that is put in writing (see Chapter 5, *Who Bears the Risk?*) between two parties; in this case, you and the one-legged bricky.

This very basic contract would be formed using the SoW, his quote, your acceptance, and basic ingredients such a as timing, programme, and the ever-important payment agreement. This can all be put together in a very simple form to suit your requirements.

You have his quote, you have by then agreed payment terms, which should be on the basis of say fortnightly valuations using the spreadsheet that you created with his items' figures, and then modified to allow for the periodic draw downs. Each time you conduct a valuation, a percentage of each item is agreed, he raises an invoice, and you pay within an agreed period of, say, seven days.

On the subject of payment, we will have covered in a different chapter, the importance of a cashflow chart in even its basic form. But having the money in place and making payments on time is of absolute importance, speaks volumes about you as an employer and believe me buys you loyalty.

Your average subbie will be prepared to do the job slightly cheaper if he knows that you pay promptly, and conversely, is quite likely to dodge off to someone else's job halfway through yours if you do not pay your bills on time and they do.

Back to the agreement, you then write back to him stating your acceptance with the agreed payment terms, including the agreed start date and expected duration of his works. This forms the second part of your contract, but subject to how far before his scheduled start date you are creating this, timings and other factors may remain to be confirmed (TBC).

Now, back to the subject of payment, there are only a few exceptions to any monies being paid in advance. A typical example would be for forward ordering of specific materials, such as windows to be timed accordingly. Generally speaking though, you should only employ a subbie who is self-supporting financially.

Even in the case of the windows, if part of a larger package with a contractor, an invoice could be raised, but you may make the payment directly to the window company, therefore keeping control of the finance but maintaining the responsibility with the contractor. Any contractor asking for 'monies up front' is speaking volumes about his credibility, but equally important, a client who is prepared to part with money before having anything to show for it also sends out a message of compliance. You are then putting him in charge of the proceedings, and not yourself.

In the case of the one-legged bricky, you may have an agreement to pay for the bricks as soon as they are delivered to site because it is a substantial sum, but this agreement must be laid out in his mini package that you are putting in place as a form of contract.

Another difficult and misconceived subject when employing subbies is that of retention. If you were to be employing a main contractor with a formal contract it is entirely likely (subject to the size of the works) that 5 per cent would be deducted from each valuation.

When practical completion is reached (at handover but with snagging items outstanding), half of the retention pot is released and the other half (2.5 per cent) is held for an agreed period of usually 6 months to cover any defects and to give certain incentives for the contractor to return and fix them.

Since I am writing this on the basis of you employing sub-contractors, there are only a couple of trades where any form of retention could be argued as appropriate. Brickworks, for example, are either complete or not, and there is little about the works that could deteriorate once deemed satisfactory. Therefore, what would you be holding a retention for?

There is a small argument for retaining monies on a plumber, as leaks could manifest a week or two after final payment, or the boiler could pack up.

Whatever the trade that you feel should offer some comfort by way of a retention, it is a subject that must be discussed, agreed, and put in writing at the time of acceptance, and therefore forms part of your mini contract package. If not, you would most definitely lose a battle in court if you withheld monies on the contractor without it being agreed in writing.

In theory, with all of the above in place, you should have your team together and be ready to get on with the works.

# 26

# Other Insurances

There are several insurance policies which need to be in place for your build:

- Structural defects warranty, that we have dealt with previously
- Site insurance, including public liability and works in progress.
- Buildings insurance, if working on an existing property

## Site Insurance, including Public Liability and Works in Progress

Building your own home involves a lot of time, effort and cash, so it's prudent to prepare in case something goes wrong. For example, what if someone was injured on site, a storm damaged the construction, or valuable tools were stolen?

It doesn't take much to throw the project off course and put you out of pocket. It is therefore essential to arrange appropriate self-build insurance cover.

A number of specialist insurers offer cover for self-build projects. Site insurance, sometimes called contract works insurance, covers a range of risks including flood, storm, and fire, and usually includes any temporary buildings on the site, such as huts and caravans, as well as the property under construction. Also, more often than not, site insurance includes any professional fees, site clearance, and debris removal in the event of a claim.

### When to take out the policy

Finding a site for your home-building project is just the first step on this highly rewarding path, but there will ultimately be a time between your purchase of the land and the commencement of building works. As you are liable for any third parties that may enter your land, such as surveyors or ground technicians, site liability insurance cover would be an option if there is likely to be a significant gap between taking ownership and works commencing, and will give you the peace of mind you need during this time. The policy will cover you in the event that somebody is injured or suffers damage or loss whilst your plot is just a plot.

### What needs to be covered

When taking out the policy, you would usually be given the facility to opt in or out of certain elements, which would affect the premium cost.

#### *Contract works*

This all-encompassing policy usually lasts for up to 18 months and includes employers' liability insurance, public liability insurance, and contractors' 'all risks' protection – in short, all the insurance elements you need to feel secure while you're building your home.

### *Theft of equipment*

Most self-build insurance policies pay out if thieves break into the site and steal any plant tools or equipment. Site insurance will also normally cover any tools and personal effects belonging to employees, though the limit is usually about £2,000. Of course, it's up to you to keep the site locked when not in use – and most insurers will insist on a high level of security to deter potential thieves.

### *Hired-in plant*

Although most plant hire companies will provide damage or theft liability waiver, there is a cost to this that would quickly outweigh the figure for inclusion to your self-build policy. Once in place, you can show the document to the hire company and not have to pay the waiver charge.

### *Responsibilities of the site owner*

If you are building your own home, you have to think about protecting more than the site and its contents. You also have to consider your liabilities, both to members of the public and to your employees (even sub-contract).

Let's say someone – even a trespasser – came onto the site and injured themselves. Or maybe a falling branch damaged a neighbour's property. As the site owner, you could be held legally responsible, which means you could end up with a big compensation bill. A self-build insurance policy will typically cover public liability up to £5 million, and you should make sure it is in place as soon as you buy the plot of land.

### *Employer's liability*

As part of the CDM regulations, you also have a legal responsibility to any employees that could include self-employed tradesmen employed by you for specific works, and you could, therefore, be liable to pay compensation, plus any costs, if an employee suffered an injury or contracted a disease as a result of working on the site.

Check the limits on your policy but most will include employer's liability up to £10 million. Remember, this is compulsory!

*Time scale*
Self-build house insurance differs from a standard policy because it typically runs for 18 months rather than 1 year. There is also normally the option to extend the cover if the project is not completed on schedule. There are usually different policy structures for those intending to live in the property as opposed to those selling it on, so best to check when taking out the cover.

*Surrounding property*
It's worth checking that your policy covers any damage to surrounding property caused by collapse, subsidence, heave, vibration, weakening or removal of support, or lowering of ground water, as a result of the works on your self-build project. Fundamentally, it depends on the nature of the works and the geology of the site, and your engineer or surveyor should be able to offer advice.

## Renovation / Loft Conversion / Extension Insurance

If you are undertaking other works to an existing property, then a different approach is required.

If you have just bought the property, then chances are you have either not insured it yet, or you have a straightforward building insurance policy. In the majority of cases, this will not cover you for the works or indeed the building whilst works are in progress.

If you are to commence works on your existing home, you cannot always rely on your existing household insurers to provide cover for the building works or indeed provide cover for the materials on site and the additional public and employee's liability exposures.

In almost all cases, you would be required to notify your present insurances that 'changes' are to take place; they may or may not then provide the cover whilst works are in progress.

Apart from the policy types mentioned previously, there are specifically designed insurances to cover your project - whether it is a short period renovation or a larger extension project - which can provide cover from only 3 months onwards. But no matter what the duration of cover, you need to include all the new works, materials on site, public and employee's liability, as well as items of plant.

# 27

# VAT

**The VAT process for the self-builder.**

The good news for self-builders and individuals who are converting a non-residential building into a home is that you can claim back most of the VAT paid out on your build.

The arrangements for reclaiming the VAT are set out in VAT notice 431NB - *VAT refunds for 'do-it-yourself' builders and converters.* The scheme only applies to those building or converting for their own domestic use and occupation, and isn't available for property developers.

The claim must be made within 3 months of the building being completed, and you only get one chance to claim, so you need to get it right the first time. You can make a claim for most of the goods and materials bought from a VAT registered supplier, which are incorporated into the building or the site.

## New Build

A new build is zero-rated, which means that a VAT registered builder or sub-contractor must zero-rate their work and not charge VAT on any labour-only or supply-and-fix contracts. Although the builder or sub-contractor will have to pay VAT when they purchase materials, they will be able to claim that back at the end of each month or the period they have agreed with HM Revenue & Customs (HMRC), and they must not seek to pass the tax on. Some smaller VAT registered contractors will be reluctant, as it can, in theory, affect their cashflow because they have to pay it out but cannot claim it back until their end of quarter.

A self-builder will have to pay VAT at full rate for the purchase of any materials that they make on their own account. This is largely recoverable at the end of the project.

## Finishing a building

You can still make a claim if you add to or finish a partly completed new building; for example, where you buy a shell from a developer and fit it out, or have it fitted out by a builder.

You cannot, however, claim for any extra work you do on a completed building bought from a builder or developer - such as adding a conservatory, patio, double-glazing, tiling, or a garage.

## Conversions

Where the building is a conversion, it must be of a non-residential building. That means a building that has either never been lived in, or hasn't been lived in for the last 10 years - not even on an occasional basis as a second home.

Unlawful occupation by squatters doesn't count, however, and you are allowed to live in the property while the work is being done, as long you move in after the work has started.

There are strict definitions with HMRC for what constitutes a suitable residential conversion, so make sure you are aware.

### Who Can Use the Scheme?

Anyone who buys eligible goods for a project that qualifies for this relief may make a claim. It doesn't matter who actually does the work - you can use builders to do some or all of it for you.

### What Goods and Services can You Claim For?

#### Goods

You can only claim for building materials. HMRC uses a strict definition for building materials. Building materials are incorporated into the building or conversion itself, or into the site, which means that you can't remove them without using tools and damaging the building and / or the goods themselves.

However, there are a number of exceptions. Items such as fitted furniture, some electrical and gas appliances, and carpets or garden ornaments do not count as building materials.

This is a really easy one to get wrong - skip hire, for example, cannot be claimed back; likewise, say, tower scaffold for the carpenter or tacker to use. It is often best to have the contractor supply certain items that cannot be reclaimed under the scheme, and then incorporate within his package and zero-rate it to you. As a rule of thumb, reclaimable items have to actually form part of the fabric of the build / site.

Scaffolding companies can also sometimes be deemed supply-and-fix companies, but aspects of the service are technically hired, which cannot be reclaimed. Many scaffold companies will zero-rate their entire invoice; but be careful when accounting this element.

I came across an interesting one recently where the client had purchased the supply and fix of concrete floor beams through his account with the builder's merchant.

The supplier was providing the beams on a supply-and-fix basis to the merchant, but because the merchant had no mechanism for zero-rating the supply to the client, VAT at standard rate was applied. However, when the client tried to reclaim the VAT through the scheme, HMRC would not allow this one because VAT should not technically have been charged in the first place as it was a supply and fix. The client lost the VAT on the whole invoice.

**Purchases abroad**
You can claim back the VAT paid on building materials bought in any member state of the EU. For the purposes of your claim, you should convert the amount of VAT you have been charged to sterling. You can also claim back the VAT paid on importing building materials into the EU. When making your claim, you must provide evidence of the VAT paid, together with the originals of any shipping or transit documents showing the importation of the goods from abroad.

**Services**
If you are constructing a new building, then your builder's services should be zero-rated anyway. You won't pay any VAT on their bill.

If you are converting a non-residential building into a home, you can reclaim the VAT charged by your builder. For conversions, a builder can sometimes charge you a reduced rate instead of the standard rate of VAT.

You cannot reclaim VAT paid on any professional or supervisory services, such as work carried out for you by architects or surveyors, or any other fees for management, consultancy, design, and planning.

## How to Make a Claim

### Timing

You can't claim as the work goes along; you have to wait until it's finished according to the original plans. If in doubt, you can wait until Building Control issues a certificate of completion.

You must make your claim within 3 months of completing your conversion or building work. If you can't, you must write to HMRC to explain the reason for the delay.

HMRC will acknowledge receipt of your claim by letter within ten working days and try to ask any questions they have about your claim at the same time. You should normally get your refund within 30 banking days of them receiving your claim.

### VAT invoices

Before you can make a claim, you need to make sure you have all the right paperwork in place. That means obtaining VAT invoices for everything, which have to be correct. If you've been charged the wrong rate of VAT, then you can't claim it. For example, if you find out you've been charged VAT in error for services that should have been zero-rated, you can't claim it back from HMRC. However, your builder may be able to obtain a VAT refund by adjusting his account with HMRC. But don't leave it until too late. Your builder will have a limited amount of time to correct his VAT account with HMRC. He is likely to refuse to make a correction if it is out of time.

VAT invoices must show:

- The supplier's VAT registration number.
- The quantity and description of the goods and / or services.
- Your name and address if the value is more than £100.
- The price of each item.

**Making the claim**
If you are constructing a new dwelling, you must complete form VAT431NB to make your claim. If you are converting a building (that was previously non-residential) into a dwelling, you must complete form VAT 431C to make your claim.

It's a lot easier to do this as you go along, so it makes sense to obtain the forms before you start work. You can download these forms, which are accompanied by guidance on how to complete them.

The notes explain the completion process step by step. They also tell you how to calculate your claim and what documents you will need to send in to support it. You should keep a copy of your claim in case HMRC need to ask you any questions about it. You must send your completed claim to the address shown in the notes that accompany the form.

**Evidence of completion**
HMRC will accept any of these as evidence that the work is finished:

- A certificate or letter of completion from the local authority, for Building Regulations purposes or otherwise
- A habitation certificate or letter from the local authority; or in Scotland, a temporary certificate of habitation

- A valuation rating or Council Tax assessment
- A certificate from your bank or building society confirming that the final completion funds have been released

Remember, this is your money, so keep every invoice and related paperwork safely documented and filed, so that as soon as the last invoice is in, you can make the claim.

# 28

# Energy Performance

Apart from straight forward energy performance measures over recent years, we have also seen designers and manufacturers needing to get their thinking caps on to design technologies that not only do the job but are also commercially competitive. The introduction of the Code for Sustainable Homes threw down the gauntlet to manufacturers and inventors to find new technologies, and whilst technically the CSH is now withdrawn by the government, I believe that the single most important effect on construction methods in recent years has been the introduction of sustainability issues.

Sustainability means considering materials, longevity, and now, crucially, $CO_2$ emissions. It means building houses that suit the young and old alike; that can be adapted to meet changing needs over generations; and that use replaceable materials. For the sustainable builder, energy efficiency is a factor within the overall design.

Energy can come from a zero-carbon source, and efficiency does not need to be the altar upon which all other things are sacrificed.

Within the construction industry, the concept of sustainability is intended to address environmental issues and build techniques in both the construction phase, and then, help improve the post-construction running cost and reduce carbon footprint. However, in my opinion, with CSH, there were many questions over practicalities for the (self) builder, and making certain aspects mandatory from a planning perspective led to more costs for ultimately the end user. It was also a minefield for the novice, requiring costly input from a licenced assessor.

The way forward, as now in place, is to make sustainability issues and implementation a part of the Building Regulations' structure. This, therefore, brings straightforward mechanics into, say, the working drawings, giving the builder without extensive sustainability experience a chance to comply without drama.

Since we have previously explained the technical considerations in Chapter 12, SAP / EPC, in this chapter, we will explore the numerous mechanical aspects which become fundamental issues when considering the design of your home, be it a new build or a re-furb.

## Passivhaus

The term **Passivhaus** (in German, meaning **passive house**) refers to a rigorous, voluntary standard for energy efficiency in a building that reduces its ecological footprint. It results in ultra-low-energy buildings that require little energy for space heating or cooling.

Passive design is not an attachment or supplement to architectural design, but a design process that is integrated within.

Although it is mostly applied to new buildings, it has also been used for refurbishments.

However, the point of Passivhaus is to reduce energy consumption – that's it. It is a design and construction method developed by Dr Wolfgang Feist over the past 20 years in Germany to reduce the amount of energy a house uses. It is not concerned with $CO_2$ emissions, with sustainable materials, with embodied energy, or embodied $CO_2$. It sets two energy benchmarks: 15kWh/m$^2$/yr for space heating and 120kWh/m$^2$/yr to include space heating, domestic hot water, lighting, fans, pumps, and main appliances. But this begs the question, is energy efficiency really all that matters?

Passivhaus is a choice. Compliance with Building Regulations Part L, for example, is mandatory across most of the country. So, if the self-builder chooses to adopt Passivhaus, they will have to do so in addition to – not instead of – meeting the prevailing Building Regulations.

The Passivhaus standard is sometimes confused with more generic approaches to passive solar architecture, with which it shares some common principles. However, the Passivhaus standard differs from more generic concepts is in its ability to reduce the permitted space heating demand and primary energy consumption. It can, therefore, be considered both as a robust energy performance specification and a holistic low-energy design concept.

With Passivhaus, thermal comfort is sought to the greatest practical extent through the use of passive measures enlisted further, which can be applied not only to the residential sector but also to commercial, industrial, and public buildings.

- Good levels of insulation with minimal thermal bridges
- Passive solar gains and internal heat sources
- Excellent level of airtightness
- Good indoor air quality, provided by a whole house mechanical ventilation system with highly efficient heat recovery

There are no strict requirements with respect to domestic hot water, lighting, and appliance consumption. The standard imposes an overall limit on the primary energy consumption, which promotes energy efficiency in all of these areas.

The Passivhaus standard's strengths lie in the simplicity of its approach: build a house that has excellent thermal performance and exceptional airtightness with mechanical ventilation.

This robust approach to building design allows the designer to minimise the heating demand of the building, and in some residential buildings, enables them to only specify a heated towel rail as means of conventional heating, this heat can then be recovered and circulated by a mechanical ventilation and heat recovery (MVHR) unit.

## Cold Bridging

Cold bridging is the term used to describe an area of a building's envelope, where a product (or products) with poor insulation properties passes through the external element. This path of low thermal resistance allows cold external temperatures to be transferred through the construction, reducing the temperature of internal surfaces. This creates a high risk of condensation forming on these cold areas.

Because insulation itself is subject to the law of diminishing returns, the first, say, 50 mm of insulation does most of the heat saving in a wall, roof, or floor. The next 50 mm saves much less, and beyond this, adding another 50 mm makes significantly less difference. At this point, other factors such as airtightness and cold bridging become far more significant, and you have to address them if you want to make the house more energy efficient.

Thermal bridges are common in older buildings, which may be poorly constructed, poorly insulated, with single-skin construction and single glazing.

In modern buildings, thermal bridging can occur because of poor design or poor workmanship. This is common where elements of the building penetrate through its insulated fabric, for example, around glazing, or where the structure penetrates the building envelope, such as at balconies.

However, buildings have become better insulated with increasingly strict regulation; so, thermal bridges that might previously have been considered insignificant in terms of the overall thermal performance of a building can actually be the cause of considerable thermal inefficiency. The potential for such inefficiency exists at every opening and every junction (even in party walls).

The most effective way of countering cold bridges is to design them out. You can't eliminate junctions and openings, but you can design them in such a way that the heat leakage at these points is minimised.

The correct design of these areas can reduce and eliminate cold bridges and their associated problems. The evolution of UK Building Regulations in recent years has seen an attempt to do this by implementing minimum design criteria in areas that are most susceptible to cold bridging.

Materials with high thermal conductivity, such as metals, transfer significantly higher quantities of heat than materials with lower thermal conductivity such as wood. Reducing thermal bridge can be as simple as material substitutions: using wood stud versus metal stud or more complex insulation strategies.

Highly conductive materials in contact with one another will increase the flow of energy – from indoors to outdoors (in cold climates) and in the opposite direction (in hot climates). Some general guidelines can be considered in reducing thermal bridges by separating highly thermal conductive materials with insulating materials; selecting less thermally conductive materials at the onset of the design; and reducing surface area in contact between highly conductive materials. Despite these general considerations, the issue of thermal bridging is almost always specific to localised areas and details, so a good understanding both during design and during

construction is required to work towards eliminating cold bridging.

## U-values, R-values, K-values

Most of you with a basic understanding of energy performance design requirements will recognise the term U-value.

In its basic form, it is a number applied to a component that helps us determine whether that component's property needs to be improved to suit the performance requirements. The most obvious modules of interest are the fabrics of the building: the walls, floor, roofs, and windows, with certain elements easier to adjust to suit than others.

**U-value**

U-value is a measure of how much heat will pass through a thermal object, such as a wall or window. A low U-value means little heat will pass through it.

U-value is measured in $W/m^2K$ – that is, Watts per square metre per degree Kelvin (1 degree Kelvin is the same as 1 degree Centigrade, but with a different zero).

So if a wall has a U-value of 1.0, then 1 $m^2$ of wall will let 1 Watt pass through it when there is a temperature difference of 1 degree between the inside and outside.

Typical limits of U-value in buildings vary from a maximum of about 5.0 $W/m^2K$ for a single-glazed window to a minimum of about 0.15 $W/m^2K$ for a modern roof with 300 mm of loft insulation – so the window lets about 30 times as much heat pass through 1 $m^2$ of it, compared to the roof.

**K-value**

The wall is called a thermal object because its U-value can be calculated from each of the components it is made of.

Each component, say the outer skin of brickwork in a cavity wall, will let heat pass through it based on two factors:

- Its thermal conductivity
- How thick it is

Thickness matters because the thicker something is, the slower the heat will pass through it – a thick jumper keeps heat in better than a thin jumper.

The thermal conductivity is a measure of how easily heat passes through the material and is called the k-value (little 'k', which helps stop confusing it with the big 'K', degrees Kelvin). K-value is measured in W/mK. Thermal conductivity is an inherent property of a material, like stiffness or density.

The U-value of a single component is given by the formula U = k/l – conductivity divided by thickness (in thermal calculation, the thickness always seems to be represented by 'l', not 't', as you might expect). So that the outer skin of brickwork, on its own, might have a thermal conductivity, k of 0.84 W/mK and a thickness of 100 mm (or 0.10 m), so U = 0.84/0.10 = 8.4 W/m$^2$K – yes, worse than a single-glazed window!

Typical limits of k-value in building materials are a maximum of around 2.0 W/mK for concrete and sandstone to a minimum of about 0.025 W/mK for polyisocyanurate (PIR) foam insulation.

**R-value**

America uses a different way of expressing resistance to heat flow, using the R-value, thermal resistance. This is just the inverse U-value, so 1/R = U. Of course, they don't use metric units, so you can't compare their R-values directly with ours.

So big R-values are more resistant to heat flow. In (European) SI units, a U-value of 0.2 will have an R-value of 5.0 m$^2$K/W and this would be equivalent to an American R-value of 28 (units are h.ft.ºF/Btu) – American R-values are 5.67 times SI R-values.

We have to use R-values in thermal calculations because we can't add up the U-values of each component in a thermal object. However, we can add up each component's value to get the total R-value (the convention is that the little r is used for the components and the big R is used for the whole thermal object).

So R = r1 + r2 + r3 + r4 and so on. Each individual r is the inverse of the U-value, so r = l/k, thickness divided by conductivity.

## U-value calculation

What follows is a sample U-value calculation for a thermal object: a cavity brick wall. This adds up the r-value of each component to get the total R-value and then takes the inverse to get the U-value.

This calculation introduces a second form of resistance to heat flow: surface resistance. Transferring heat from, for example, the air right against the wall in a room into the plaster of the wall creates a resistance to heat flow, so these boundaries behave a bit like zero-thickness insulation.

| Component | Thickness<br>l<br>mm | Thermal conductivity<br>k<br>W/mK | Thermal resistance<br>r = l / k<br>m2K/W |
|---|---|---|---|
| Outer surface | - | - | 0.04 |
| Outer leaf of brickwork | 100 | 0.75 | 0.13 |
| Cavity | - | - | 0.18 |
| Inner leaf of blockwork | 100 | 0.55 | 0.18 |
| Plaster | 15 | 0.50 | 0.03 |
| Inner surface | - | - | 0.13 |
| Total, R | | | 0.70 |
| | | | |
| U-value = 1/R (in W/m2K) | | | 1.44 |

This example shows that surface resistance is quite important – it is exactly half of the total resistance of this cavity wall.

The cavity itself is entered as a surface resistance, since the air is free to move around inside the cavity (by convection); so the main resistance comes from the two boundaries.

Since the majority of us rely on the U-value to provide a recognisable figure when choosing say the correct window to incorporate in the build in relation to other components, it has become the universal illustrating value.

## Airtightness and its Advantages

Why is it important to get airtightness right?

'Build tight, ventilate right'. For a long time now, this song has been the rallying cry of energy-efficiency experts; but until recently, it seemed to be landing on deaf ears.

To many in the UK, the concept of airtightness seems somehow alien and unwelcome. 'I don't want to live in a sealed box' is a typical response, or 'I always sleep with the windows open, so what's the point?' They fear that an airtight house will be an unhealthy one, full of stale smells and condensation. Indeed, the classic Victorian house was designed to be as air-leaky as possible in order to expel the coal smoke: with rattling sash windows, draughts through the floorboards, and open fireplaces. This, we thought, was healthy. But perceptions have changed.

Now, with the growing awareness of concepts like Passivhaus and zero-carbon homes, people are realising just how important airtightness is in low-energy houses.

In an airtight house, air quality isn't down to random draughts; the 'ventilate right' bit of the equation has to be planned. Airtight homes rely on whole-house ventilation systems.

We thus have three essential elements to a low-energy home: lots of insulation; airtightness; and a whole-house ventilation system. The first won't work without the second; the second won't work without the third; and if you combine all three, you get a low-energy, comfortable home with good indoor air quality.

## Testing Airtightness

Airtightness is measurable. To test for it, you remove the front door and replace it – temporarily – with a blower door, which pumps air into the house, putting it under a small pressure load of 50 Pascals. This measures how much air is needed to be pumped in to keep the house at a steady 50 Pascals. The air leakage measurements are scored in cubic metres of air moving every hour through a square metre of the building envelope under 50 Pascals of pressure, often shortened to just q50. It doesn't relate to what happens in practice because homes aren't under pressure like this, but the figure does give a useful way of comparing how leaky a house is. And, in practice, it also tells us how well a house has been designed and built. It's a sort of quality mark.

The Building Regulations in England and Wales state that an airtightness pass score is 10 q50. That's not very difficult to beat, and a pass score of 10 q50 could in no way be described as an airtight house. There is, in any event, a dispensation for sites with just one or two homes. Here, you can forgo the air pressure test, but you will have to assume a score of 15 q50, which will upset your dwelling emission rate calculations and require you to install better insulation and take other energy-efficiency measures to offset heat losses. It may well be cheaper to have a test done, and, if you are aiming for an airtight house, then the test really is essential. In the rare event of a test failure, remedial steps can often be undertaken at the time of the test.

10 q50 is not a high standard and can generally be easily met by careful draught-proofing and the application of mastic here and there. A score below 3 q50 is reckoned to be pretty good, and this is the level where mechanical ventilation starts to become a necessity. The gold standard of low-energy house building - Passivhaus - demands an airtightness score of just 0.6 q50.

### Designing Airtightness In

The key to getting a good score in an airtightness test is to design in an air barrier at the outset, and then to ensure that it is properly installed and not tampered with during construction. For instance, instead of allowing plumbers to drill holes wherever they like, the service connections should be planned in advance and the air barrier penetrations sealed accordingly.

### Heating an Airtight House

The good news is that the better insulated and more airtight a house, the less heating it needs, as it is able to hold on to heat generated by day-to-day activities of the occupants. But building airtight is bad news for lovers of traditional open fires - they allow far too much air leakage to be a viable option. Wood burning stoves with an attachment that lets you draw air from outside are popular; however, they are still not truly room sealed, and every time you open the door to refuel, you upset the airflow balance and release some smoke into the room. However, as an accompaniment to underfloor heating on just the coldest days, it's not a bad solution. As airtight houses rely on whole-house ventilation anyway, the introduction of heat recovery to a mechanical system that controls air changes is a popular strategy.

However, airtightness without the correct ventilation will lead to condensation issues.

## Condensation and its Issues

So what is condensation and what causes it? Basically, condensation occurs when water, which is already in the air, settles on a colder surface and makes it damp or wet. Over time, this moisture can lead to damage by peeling paint off windows and walls.

Condensation on windows causes flaking paint around window frames and window sills. Flaking paint is a common symptom of condensation.

The damp conditions also encourage the growth of mould spores, which thrive in these moist places. This often leads to black sooty mould on windows, but you might also notice mould on walls, and even on curtains, where condensation has been allowed to build up over time.

All air contains water vapour, but the amount of water air can hold is determined by the temperature of that air. This ratio is called relative humidity. Hot air is able to carry much more moisture than cold air, so as the temperature of air rises, it is able to hold a greater volume of water. The water vapour comes from everyday activities, including bathing, cooking, and washing. Even our breathing causes condensation, and this is why car windows steam up when you sit with the windows closed and the fan off.

Once the air is saturated with water vapour (at any given temperature), it will deposit beads of water (condensation) on any surface that is cold enough. The temperature of the surface at which this moisture will form is called the dew point.

(For an example, take a cold glass bottle out of the fridge, and it will soon become wet. When the weather is hot the condensation can literally run off the bottle.)

Another area that you often see this happening on is bathroom pipes. The cold mains-water comes into a warm bathroom where the water vapour in the steamy room condenses on the pipe, often leaving a puddle of water below it. This can be so bad that you might think you have a water leak from the pipe.

Condensation forms on cold pipes in kitchens and bathrooms leading to flaking and discoloured paint. You can see this effect outside, too. Where the dew point is close to the ground, a small layer of damp air, dew, or frost is formed. Where a larger amount of air is involved, mist or fog arises. If this happens to air that is rising in the atmosphere, and therefore expanding, then clouds will form.

**If this happens in the home, it is called condensation.**

Enlisted here are the symptoms of condensation in the order they are most likely to occur – in other words, in the places most at risk of condensation forming and the way the condensation affects that area:

- Beads of water on windows
- Pools of water on the window sill
- Beads of water on external walls
- Damp patches on external walls
- Damp patches on ceilings
- Damp patches in the corners of rooms
- Damp internal walls

- Black mould on window frames, window recesses, and window sills
- Black mould on walls – particularly corners and recesses with little air flow
- Black mould in cupboards
- Black mould on curtains and clothes
- Wet internal walls

## Diagnosing Condensation

Is it rising damp or condensation? Let us look at the rising damp myth, which is that all damp at low levels must be rising damp. Let's be clear here: it is rarely rising damp; it is usually condensation, although it can also be penetrating damp – where water is getting in through damaged or shoddily built areas such as through a roof leak, cracked render, failed wall ties, damaged brickwork, or badly fitted window frames. Rising damp may occur in certain circumstances, but it is very rare in modern housing.

## Preventing Condensation

Now we have defined condensation, you know what the problem is, and what the symptoms are. The next thing you want to know is how to prevent condensation. Put simply, ventilation is the cure.

## How do I Stop Condensation?

As soon as warm air containing vapour hits a cooler surface, it will condense. This is most obvious on windows, mirrors, and wall tiles, but condensation on walls and ceilings also occurs frequently, and goes quite unnoticed.

A major no-no is the drying of damp clothes over a radiator. As the clothes are drying, the moisture from them has to go somewhere. Without ventilation, it goes directly into the air.

'If we insulate our homes and warm the house thoroughly, then this should not happen', I hear you cry. But it will!

The only way to prevent condensation is to provide ventilation. The warm air containing the water vapour will rise and circulate around the room until it finds a cooler surface, unless we let that air out and some cooler air in.

In order to ensure that there is good ventilation in your home, a change of air is recommended in all rooms of the house once a day, at the very least. Improved ventilation can help prevent condensation forming and aid in resolving problems like wet internal walls and black mould issues.

## Tips to Stop Condensation

Effective condensation control is all about lifestyle; once you get the situation under control, you will start automatically putting into place the measures that will prevent condensation from forming.

**Here is a quick guide to condensation prevention:**

- Do not push furniture right up against the walls, especially external walls, which are often the coldest in a room. Keeping furniture a little further away from the walls means the air has a free flow around the room.

- Ventilate your house - change the air once a day. Open a window or fit trickle vents. Where you have trickle vents fitted, make sure you leave them open.

- Don't dry washing indoors; if you have a tumble dryer, make sure it is properly vented or buy a self-condensing model.
- Do not fill cupboards to bursting point – again, allow the air to flow.
- Make sure that your loft insulation is not blocking the ventilation provided by the gap between the facia boards and the house wall. In modern houses, there are often purpose-made ventilation grilles and vents in the loft or breathable sarking felt.
- Install cavity wall insulation to help eliminate cold spots on internal walls. You must first ensure this complies with Building Regulations for your home.
- Have central heating or underfloor heating fitted if possible.
- Have heating thermostatically controlled wherever possible.
- Ventilate tumble driers externally, or have a self-condensing model.
- Install extractor fans in the kitchen and bathroom. The best models are available with a humidistat control, which means they are automatically triggered to operate when the humidity in the room rises.
- Install trickle vents in your windows.
- If you already have trickle vents, make sure you open them for the majority of the day to allow a change of air and improve ventilation in the home.

- Install mechanical ventilated heat recovery (MVHR). This is a whole house extract / ventilating system (explained further).

## Mechanical Ventilation

### Mechanical Ventilation and Heat Recovery (MVHR):

Is a (usually) whole house ventilating system, used more and more frequently now we are building houses with stringent levels of airtightness.

It's important for your property to breathe, especially when it's super insulated and airtight for maximum energy efficiency.

But if breathing means dumping warm air to replace it with cold air just to remove moisture, dust, and odours, there has to be a better more efficient way to ventilate a building.

### How MVHR Works

Typically, 20 per cent to 30 per cent of your space heating energy is lost through natural ventilation: trickle vents in windows, extractor fans in wet rooms, open doors, or other gaps in the building fabric. By sealing up the leaks and making your property more airtight, the flow of air can be more effectively controlled.

The MVHR system uses super-efficient fans to feed fresh, filtered air into living / working / sleeping areas, at the same time pulling stale, moist air from kitchens, bathrooms, and other indoor wet areas. The pressure differential gently controls the direction of the flow to provide fresh air where you need it.

The heat exchanger inside the MVHR then recovers up to 90 per cent of the warmth from the stale air before it leaves the building, transferring it from the old air to the new as it enters. You get fresh filtered air throughout your home without the excessive heat loss associated with traditional extract ventilation.

With the spiralling costs of energy, the need to conserve heat and power in the home is increasingly important. As we continually strive towards an airtight, super-insulated building envelope in a bid to stop our heat from escaping, we find ourselves living in a space where improved ventilation is essential.

Without adequate ventilation, contaminants such as ammonia, acetic acid, methane, nitrogen monoxide, VOCs from paints, and formaldehyde from cleaning products, not to mention the dust, odours, $CO_2$ and water vapour we produce each day, all linger in our homes and affect the health of our families. Indeed, the need for controlled ventilation is so important that a section of the Building Regulations, Part F, is devoted to the issue.

To improve airtightness only to then ventilate the property by opening windows is nonsense. Why rely on natural ventilation when heat recovery ventilation can swap stale air for fresh air without wasting energy?

An MVHR draws stale moist air from kitchens, bathrooms, and utility rooms into a heat exchanger, then uses the energy to gently blow warmed fresh air into bedrooms and living spaces. In a well-insulated building, a heat exchanger transfers up to 90 per cent of the energy from the old air to the new, reducing overall space heating bills, and at the same time, improving air quality. Further savings are made by removing the need for opening window casements, extractor fans, and trickle vents. Dry air also costs a lot less to heat than damp air.

Here is a basic diagram of how the system works:

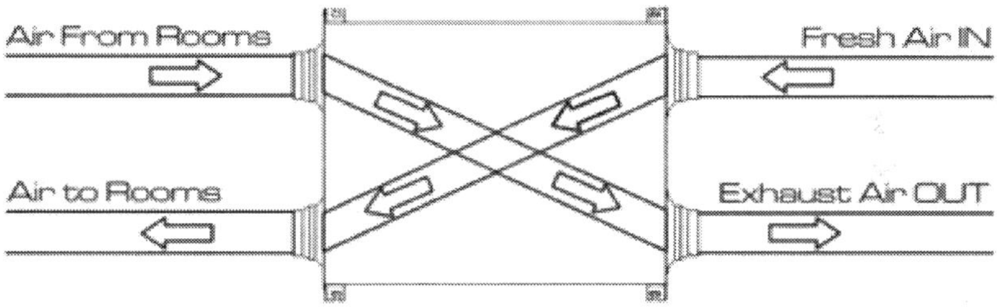


Normally consuming less electricity than a light bulb, an MVHR system creates an always-on low-pressure air movement throughout the whole property. An MVHR system should pay for itself through energy savings in around 5 years and have a working life in excess of 10, if not 20, years. Of all the energy-saving products in the market, MVHRs are generally regarded to offer the greatest return on investment. They're good for your health, your wallet, and the environment.

# 29

# Sustainability and Renewables

## Renewable Technologies

Renewable energy is derived from natural sources that are replenished constantly and will not run out. In its various forms, it derives directly from the Sun, or from heat generated deep within the earth. Included in the definition is electricity and heat generated from solar, wind, ocean, hydropower, biomass, geothermal resources, and biofuels and hydrogen derived from renewable resources.

Unlike the burning of fossil fuels that emit carbon dioxide into the atmosphere, these 'clean' energies do not release substances that are harmful to the environment. Renewable energy technologies include solar power, wind power, hydroelectricity, and biofuels.

Here is a brief outline of the different types of renewable energy.

## Solar Energy

Solar energy refers to the utilisation of energy from the Sun. Solar energy can be converted into other forms of energy, such as heat and electricity.
This form of energy can be applied in many ways, which have been described as follows.

### Solar panels

Solar panels are an ideal source of renewable energy as they are pollution free. They produce electricity quietly, unlike the energy produced from the use of fossil fuels and some other types of renewable energy which can be noisy.

Solar energy can enable electricity production in remote locations that are not linked to a national grid.

### Solar electricity

Solar photovoltaic (PV) panels generate electricity from the Sun's energy. Solar electricity is then either used to run the household electrical appliances, or it is fed back into the national grid. A generation meter is installed to monitor the volume of electricity generated by the solar photovoltaic system.

Solar PV panels are installed on the roof; the panels generate DC electricity, which is run to an inverter that converts this to usable AC current. The electricity is then passed through a total generation meter that records every unit of electricity produced by the solar PV panels. The electricity then runs to the fuse board, and from here, any electricity produced will power your household electrical appliances.

As electricity is generated, if you do not use the electricity, it will be fed back into the national grid.

How solar PV panels work:

1. Sun's energy is absorbed by PV panels on roof.
2. Energy is converted to electricity by inverter.
3. Electricity is fed through a meter.
4. Electricity is used to power domestic appliances.
5. Unused electricity is fed into the national grid.

**Solar water heating**

Solar tubes are secured to the roof with reflector plates to maximise the absorption of UV light. A heat transfer fluid is pumped around the solar circuit, which passes around the coil in your cylinder and heats the water. A solar controller is installed to regulate and control the temperature of the solar collectors and hot water cylinder.

The solar hot water heating system includes a new twin coil hot water cylinder. The bottom coil is connected to the solar panel circuit, which heats the water in your cylinder whilst energy is being produced. The top coil is connected to your existing boiler or immersion heater. The cylinder will first use the energy from the solar circuit to heat the water in your cylinder. It will then call upon your boiler or immersion if it requires extra heat to get the cylinder to its required temperature.

How solar water heating works:

1. Fluid is pumped to the solar tubes on the roof.
2. The Sun's energy warms the fluid passing through the tubes.

3. The fluid then passes through a coil in your cylinder heating the water.
4. The second coil is connected to your boiler to bring the water up to temperature.
5. The heated water is then used whenever you open a hot tap.

## Wind Energy

Wind energy is the kinetic energy that is present in moving air. This kinetic energy of the wind can be changed into other forms of energy, such as mechanical or electrical energy. Wind energy is a pollution-free, infinitely sustainable form of energy. It doesn't use fuel, it doesn't produce greenhouse gasses, and it doesn't produce toxic or radioactive waste.

### Wind turbines

Generate electricity at home with small-scale wind turbines. Wind turbines harness the power of the wind and use it to generate electricity. Forty per cent of all the wind energy in Europe blows over the UK, making it an ideal country for domestic turbines (known as microwind or small-wind turbines). A typical system in an exposed site could easily generate more power than your lights and electrical appliances use.

### Cut your electricity bills

Wind is free, so once you've paid for the initial installation, your electricity costs will be reduced.

### Get paid for what you generate

Through feed-in tariffs, you get paid for the electricity you generate even if you use it.

What you don't use, you can export to the local grid - and get paid for that too.

**Cut your carbon footprint**
Wind electricity is green, renewable energy and doesn't release any harmful carbon dioxide or other pollutants.

**Store electricity for a calm day**
If your home isn't connected to the national grid, you can now store excess electricity in batteries and use it when there is no wind.

## Biomass

Biomass is produced from organic materials derived from living organisms or from metabolic by-products (organic or food waste products), such as wood, woodchips, paper, trash, agricultural crops, animal waste, manure, sewage, hemp, and algae.
Biomass contains stored energy from the Sun, as plants use photosynthesis to grow and produce biomass. When burned, the chemical energy in biomass is released as heat. If you have a fireplace, the wood you burn is a biomass fuel. Wood waste or garbage is burned to produce steam to make electricity and to provide heat to industries and homes.

Also known as biomatter, biomass can be used directly as fuel or to produce liquid biofuel. Agriculturally produced biomass fuels such as biodiesel and ethanol can be burned in internal combustion engines or boilers.

**Biofuels**
Biofuel is any fuel derived from biomass and is a renewable energy source. The two types of biofuels are ethanol and

biodiesel. Biofuels can help reduce air toxic emissions, greenhouse gas build up, and dependence on fossil fuels. They are commonly used to power vehicles and cooking stoves.

Biofuels offer the possibility of producing energy without a net increase of carbon into the atmosphere because the plants used to produce the fuel have removed $CO_2$ from the atmosphere during growth, unlike fossil fuels, which return carbon that was stored beneath the Earth's surface for millions of years into the air. Biofuel is therefore more carbon-neutral and less likely to increase atmospheric concentrations of greenhouse gases. The use of biofuels also reduces dependence on petroleum.

## Geothermal Heat Pumps

Geothermal heat pumps (GHPs) use the constant temperature of the Earth as the exchange medium instead of the outside air temperature. A geothermal heat pump uses the Earth's ability to store heat in the ground and water thermal masses to produce heating or air conditioning.

These systems operate based on the stability of underground temperatures: the ground, a few feet below surface, has a very stable temperature throughout the year depending upon the location's annual climate. A geothermal heat pump uses the available heat in the winter and puts heat back into the ground in the summer.

Ground-source heat pumps work by extracting heat from outside and transferring it either to the hot water or heating systems of the house, or both. The best way to visualise the process is to imagine how a fridge extracts heat from within and expels it through the elements at the back.

In the case of heat pumps, the mechanism draws heat from outside, boosts the temperature by compression and releases the heat into the property.

**How does a ground source heat pump work?**
Ground source heat pumps circulate fluid through pipes buried in the ground to extract the latent heat from the ground.

In the UK, the average temperature of the ground just below the surface is between 8 °C and 13 °C. This temperature remains fairly constant throughout the year.

The temperature of the water in the pipes is lower than the surrounding ground and so it warms up slightly. The returning water is chilled back down by a heat pump, where it is used to heat up a refrigerant. By compressing this 'warmed' refrigerant the temperature is further increased before being transferred to the building heating system. The heating water output from the heat pump is typically 45 °C – 55 °C. This process can be reversed, using the ground as a heat sink, to provide cooling water for the building.

Loops are buried in the garden. If you have lots of land, these can be horizontal loops extending over 50–100 m lengths. If you don't have lots of land, these can be vertical loops, going up to 100 m down.

The ground source unit must be located inside the house. The flow from the heat pump is divided into two: one feed goes into the hot water circuit, and one feed into the space heating system (for example, radiators / under-floor heating).

At any one moment, the heat pump feeds heat either into the hot water system or into the space heating system. It does not feed both simultaneously. A valve determines whether the heat flows into the hot water system or the space heating system.

This valve is operated by a timer, which can be set by the preferences of the user.

## Air Source Heat Pump

Air source heat pumps provide highly efficient heating and hot water for domestic homes. The intelligent controls regulate the heating automatically to not only substantially reduce energy bills but also to provide a more comfortable style of heating when compared to conventional fossil fuel boilers (gas, oil, and so on).

The system utilises the low-grade free heat from the air outside. The energy is upgraded using a sophisticated vapour compression cycle to usable temperatures that can heat your home and water.

An air source heat pump installation typically consists of an outdoor heat exchanger, an indoor hot water storage cylinder, some controls, and circulation pumps. The outdoor unit looks much like a typical air conditioning system.

Air source heat pumps can provide heat for under floor heating, standard radiators, domestic hot water, skirting board radiators.

They operate at more than three times the efficiency of conventional heating systems and, as a result, help to minimise $CO_2$ emissions and reduce the heating costs of your property.

This type of pump works all year round, even when the temperature outside is below freezing. The heat generated can also be used to heat your swimming pool.

## Water Source Heat Pump

Water source heat pumps use the energy stored in a water source to heat your home and provide hot water all year round.

Pipes are submerged in a river, stream, or lake where temperatures remain at a relatively constant level of between 7 °C and 12 °C.

Water source heat pumps can be installed as either an open or closed loop system. An open loop system uses ground water from a lake or well. In an open loop system, water is extracted and fed directly into the heat pump where the energy raised through compression is extracted as heat. This increased heat is transferred by the heat exchanger to your property's heating / hot water system where it is readily available for use. In this type of installation, you may need environment agency consent to extract and discharge water from these sources.

A closed loop system uses a refrigerant in a closed loop to transfer energy / heat from the water source, for example, a lake. Pipes are laid in a lake in which a liquid refrigerant absorbs the water's heat and transfers this heat to a heat pump located inside the house.

Virtually maintenance-free and silent to run, water source heat pumps are able to produce more energy than they consume, with every 1kW used, providing up to 4kW of energy– a huge increase from traditional electric heating, which provides just 0.9kW from 1kW of energy used, losing energy in transfer. The water source heat pump's high increase in energy delivers a very efficient form of heating. A particular benefit of these pumps is that the water sources maintain a fairly constant temperature, so the systems perform well all year round.

# 30

# Neighbours and Keeping them On Side

Just a short chapter on the subject of neighbours.

If you have bought a plot or building with planning approval previously granted, in an urban or semi-rural area, there is a serious chance that the project is met with resistance from your neighbours in the form of objections at the application stage.

This is an unfortunate fact, as people in this country inherently oppose change to what they perceive as 'their' territory, and the issue becomes worse, as local authorities are more likely to grant permission for a new dwelling in an existing built-up area; hence, the term 'backyard developments'.

Although you have bought your dream plot in good faith, blindly oblivious to any opposition, you will be the bringer of all evil and certainly a candidate for the next public flogging the day you start works.

I have, over the past year alone, been at the pointy end of some serious attitude on three occasions when building with clients; so be cautious.

On one particular build – in let's just say Berkshire – my client had bought a back garden plot with planning for a small two-bed bungalow. Unbeknown to him, the planning application had come across such serious opposition that a local resident's committee had lobbied the local authority, not quite burning down the town hall, but certainly making a huge fuss. The first we knew of it was when I wrote to the immediate neighbours either side requesting permission for Thames Water to lift drainage chambers to inspect with CCTV cameras, and at the same time introducing myself as the client's project manager.

Not only did I receive stark refusal, but this kick-started a barrage of emails from the chairman of the residents' association, first to inform me of the opposition, and then to let me know quite blatantly that he would be making my life a misery. (Hello Ted! – In the unlikely event that you are reading this book, you know who you are!)

What followed was nothing short of harassment, with visits from planners, Building Control, Thames Water (clean water and sewer), highways, and even the police.

The final straw came when the Chartered Institute of Building (CIOB) wrote to me informing me that they had received a letter of complaint, suggesting that I was perhaps not worthy of membership, as I had organised the connection of the foul sewer to the surface water drainage! (clearly I had not).

Needless to say, I explained myself and the trouble with certain neighbours, so I kissed and made up with CIOB, but it was a nuisance nevertheless.

Granted this was an extreme situation, but do not underestimate the locals. As a matter of course with all sites, new build or re-furb, I write to the immediate natives introducing myself as point of contact in all circumstances and giving them as much general information regarding the proposed works and the duration of the likely disruption.

I explain that consideration for them is paramount, there are strict site rules, disturbance will be kept to a minimum, but unfortunately, construction works are generally a bit noisy and dusty.

This simple act is usually well received and is an investment. If you are new to the plot, you can glean very important information from the neighbours, so being on side with them is an absolute must.

Then there is the subject of site security. Ironically, the same curtain twitcher who is the first out there asking you to move contractors' vehicles parked in front of his / her drive, which has not had a car on it for a month, will be the first to call you or the police if a suspicious someone is seen wandering about the site after hours. Neighbourhood watch takes on a whole new level with nosy citizens.

Of course, it is entirely likely that you will need to be in contact and require co-operation regarding any Party Wall Agreement (see Chapter 16, *Party Wall*) with either side, but opposite neighbours are also useful allies. You need them too, so put your metaphorical arm around them as well (or they will park right opposite your site entrance so you cannot get deliveries in and out).

However, it is just as likely that the neighbours will welcome the development, offer all manners of useful information, bring you and the workers cups of tea, and guard your build like a Doberman when you are not there, but .......?

# 31

# And Finally...

Hopefully, you now have all the tools and insight in your possession to go out there and manage the pre-construction phase of your project.

As I said at the beginning, it is entirely possible that I have not covered every single element that you have to address. However, with the knowledge and understanding of the mechanics, you should have the confidence and attitude to tackle the project and provide the necessary cohesion.

I wish you good luck with your works.

In my second book due later this year, **The Self-builders Guide to Project Management – The Construction Phase**, I will continue through the preparation of the site, the need for pre-start meetings, and general tips on the numerous trades and what to address and look out for.

Turn the page for a brief excerpt from one of the chapters on trades elements.

* * *

# Excerpt from my exciting second volume

## The Self-builders Guide to Project Management - The Construction Phase

### Demolition

Let's assume for the sake of this chapter that you are demolishing an existing building to make way for the construction of your new house.

My first words of advice would be: do not consider this yourself! Although on the face of it, the works seem simple enough, there are a whole host of legislative and health and safety hoops to jump through. Without these necessary documents in place, will land you the wrong side of Building Control, Department of Environment (DoE), Health and Safety Executive (HSE), not to mention the police, to name but a few. There are very strict laws regarding waste carrier licences and landfill tax that dictate heavily what may or may not happen to the material when you have dropped the building, with, in some cases, the need for the site to be registered with DoE.

Not only that, demolition in its basic form is an extremely dangerous aspect requiring expert and professional procedures.

You may think that by perching yourself and a mate on ladders and removing the roof tiles yourself for reuse or even to sell, you will make or save a few quid – but if the tiles have a value, it is far better to negotiate it with a demolition company when quoting than run the risk of hurting yourself or being prosecuted. Having said that, if you have items of value, like fireplaces or that 200-year-old grand oak staircase, then clearly, it is worth removing it before handing the building over to the demolition company. Taking the bother to remove cable or pipe work for its minuscule scrap value is, in my opinion, a waste of effort versus gain. You will certainly not save any money with the demolition company's quote by stripping out part of the interior yourself.

So, assuming that you have decided to take the sensible route and employed a demolition company, you will previously have agreed with them as to who will provide welfare facilities (Portaloo?), but other than that they should be self-sufficient.

Bear in mind my comments in the VAT chapter of Vol 1 about reclaiming VAT on hired items and including items such as a toilet or container hire in someone's package.

To begin with, whoever actually razes the building to the ground, would at the very least need to be armed with an asbestos survey. All decent demo companies will insist on it because as licensed waste carriers, they will have to tick certain boxes with DoE and wherever they are disposing of the waste. It's not so much about identifying any asbestos but more about proving its existence and, therefore, what happens to it. In the event that there are no asbestos-based materials found in the building, they would need to prove that as well, so there would be no question of any in the waste when taken away.

If, for example, a bat survey was specified at planning approval stage, the results and any subsequent action will be needed by demo firm for their file.

You will also have provided them with the CDM Pre-Construction Information (PCI) pack that we have covered in a different chapter on Construction (Design and Management).

In return, the demolition company will provide you with their risk assessment and method statement for your CDM construction phase plan.

They will want confirmation (often in writing) that all main utility services are disconnected. When all of this is in place, stand back!

Different-sized companies have different ways of going forward. If they feel that any salvageable materials are involved, they will no doubt strip them out by hand. In some cases, if the house was built using a valuable brick or roof tile on the reclaim market, then they too will be separated, cleaned, palleted, and taken away. This will, of course, have been taken into consideration at quoting stage, and I have known circumstances where the demo company will take the building down at no cost in exchange for the salvageable materials - but that is rare!

In most cases though, a large machine - 20 tonnes or thereabouts with a hydraulic grab on the end - will simply pull the building over, separating the inert materials from the non-inert. Usually, the inert is taken away in six wheelers whereas the non-inert is put in large roll-on-roll-off (ROLO) skips for disposal, and that's where the documents discussed earlier in this section come in.

Quite often, I would ask them to track in some of the hardcore as a hard standing area for deliveries or parking, which, especially if building superstructure during the winter, will come in very handy later and will cost no money.

You will expect Demo co, as part of their brief, to be grubbing up and carting away all foundations and obsolete drainage, and then backfilling with rubble / finings and tracking into compact. In many cases, you will be rebuilding in a similar area; so the more you track in and compact the ground, the less likelihood of foundations, when dug, becoming larger than you want or even caving in, with the obvious cost of extra concrete and other materials.

Make sure that they leave the entire area flat and level before calling it complete.

Now on a slightly separate but related note, if you are doing any ground sculpting or reducing or raising general ground levels, it is usually far more cost effective to have the demo company include it within their package, as they will already have the plant on site. Likewise, if the top soil is to be removed and put to one side, to be brought back later by landscapers, then get the demo company to do it within their works. Remember, moving material about is cheaper for them than taking it away. One thing to consider with this element is that it happens very quickly; in most cases, I would expect a decent demolition company to be in, drop and clear away a reasonably sized detached house, and be gone in a week or so.

------------------------------

Sign up for my newsletter at www.vinceholden.com to receive regular updates on the release date of my next book, along with other valuable articles and notifications.
* To contact me for free advice, send me an email at the following address:

vinc@vinceholden.com

# Glossary

Since, inherently, we tend to use abbreviations and acronyms, I thought it best to give a brief explanation of each one.

**ACD** - Accredited Construction Details - performance standards required to demonstrate compliance with the energy efficiency requirements (Part L) of the Building Regulations.

**ACM** – Asbestos Containing Materials

**ARB** – Architects Registration Board

**ASHP** - Air Source Heat Pump - is a system which transfers heat from outside to inside a building, or vice versa, under the principles of vapour compression refrigeration.

**BoQ** – Bill of Quantities - is a document used in tendering whre materials, parts, and labour are quantified, itemized and costed.

**BR** - Building Regulations.

**BRE** - Building Research Establishment is a former UK government establishment (but now a private organisation) that carries out research, consultancy and testing for the construction sectors in the United Kingdom.

**BREEAM (BREDEM)** - Building Research Establishment Environmental Assessment Methodology - sets the standard for best practice in sustainable building design, construction and operation and has become one of the most comprehensive and widely recognised measures of a building's environmental performance.

**CAD (Autocad)** - AutoCAD is a computer-aided drafting software program used for creating blueprints for buildings. Usually creates files in dwg format

**CDM** - Construction Design & Management (Health & Safety) – See chapter

**CIAT** - Chartered Institute of Architectural Technologists - is the lead qualifying body for Architectural Technology and represents those practising and studying within the discipline.

**CIOB** - Chartered Institute of Building - is the world's largest and most influential professional body for construction management and leadership.

**CISE** - Chartered Institution of Structural Engineers - is the world's leading professional body for qualifications and standards in structural engineering.

**CLS** - Canadian Lumber Standard - was originally manfactured in Canada for use in the building of **timber** framed houses, hence it's name.

Over the past few years **CLS** has become increasingly popular in the UK for use as framing for stud walls and internal partitions.

**CSH** - Code for Sustainable Homes - is the national standard for the sustainable design and construction of new homes.

**DER/ TER** - The Dwelling Emission Rate (*DER*) and the Target Emission Rate (*TER*) are the headline Co2 figures which SAP Calculations measure.

**DOE** – Department Of the Environment

**DPC** – Damp Proof Course

**DPM** – Damp Proof Membrane

**ECD** - Enhanced Construction Details – next generation of ACD's (see above)

**EL Insurance** – Employers Liability Insurance

**EPC** – Energy Performance Certificate - gives a property an energy efficiency rating from A (most efficient) to G (least efficient) and is valid for 10 years.

**EU** – European Union

**F10** – Notification form to HSE

**FDN** – FounDatioN - concrete mix

**FRA** - Flood Risk Assessment

**FSC** - Forest Stewardship Council - certificate verifies forest products along the production chain of processing and transformation, and ensures that the timber is sourced from a sustainable location.

**GSHP** - Ground Source Heat Pump

**HMRC** – Her Majesty's Revenue and Customs

**HSE** – Health and Safety Executive

**HVAC** - Heating Ventilating Air Conditioning

**ICF** – Insulated Concrete Formwork

**IDDA** - Interior Decorators and Designers Association.

**JCT** - Joint Contracts Tribunal - produces standard forms of **contract** for construction, guidance notes and other standard documentation for use in the construction industry.

**LABC** – Local Authority Building Control - represent building control teams in councils across England, but also confusingly is the name of LABC Warranty, a private company who work in partnership with Local Authority

**LPA** - Local Planning Authority

**LPG** - Liquified Petroleum Gas - also referred to as simply propane or butane.

**MDPE** – Medium-Density Polythene – usually used for underground water or gas pipe

**MMC** – Modern Methods of Construction

**MPAN** - Meter Point Administration Number, also know as Supply Number or S-Number, is a 21-digit reference used to uniquely identify electricity supply points such as individual domestic residences.

**MPRN** - Meter Point Reference Number – gas equivalent of the above.

**Mr & Mrs SB** – Mr & Mrs Self-Builder

**MVHR** – Mechanical Ventilation Heat recovery - see chapter

**NPPF** - National Planning Policy Framework

**NHBC** – National House Builders Council – Usually associated with Structural Warranty insurance

**OSB** - Oriented Strand Board also known as sterling board, sterling board, is an engineered wood particle **board** formed by adding adhesives and then compressing layers of wood strands (flakes) in specific orientations.

**P&O** – Profits and Overheads

**PC sum** - Prime Cost Sum - is the cost of an item that has either not been selected or the price was unknown at the time the contact was entered into, but will be eventually nominated by the client

**Prov Sum** - Provisional sum - is an allowance, usually estimated, that is inserted into tender documents for a specific element of the works that is not yet defined in enough detail for tenderers to price. This, together with a brief description, allows tenderers to apply mark up and attendance costs within their overall tender price.

**PD - Permitted Development**

**PI insurance** - Professional Indemnity Insurance - is provided by a professional to cover compensation he or she may need to pay to correct a mistake or cover any legal costs due to negligence, such as giving incorrect advice or making a mistake in your work.

**PM** - Project Manager

**PUR/PIR** - Rigid polyurethane (PUR) and polyisocyanurate (PIR) insulation - products are highly effective, lightweight and many have the ability to bond to most materials. Found commonly in Rigid insulation boards and SIP panels, but also now as adhesives.

**QS** – Quantity Surveyor – Creates amongst other things the BoQ (above)

**RIBA** - Royal Institute of British Architects - is a professional body for architects (see chapter).

**RICS** – Royal Institute of Chartered Surveyors - is a professional body that accredits professionals within the land, property and construction sectors.

**Robust Details** – is a set of details created in response to the housebuilding industry's request for an alternative to pre-completion sound testing as a means of satisfying the sound insulation requirements of the building regulations (in England and Wales).

**SAP** - Standard Assessment Procedure - is the calculation that is required in order to produce a Predicted Energy Assessment and a Energy Performance Certificate.

**Section 106** - The council can enter into a Section 106 agreement, otherwise known as a 'planning obligation', with a developer where it is necessary to provide contributions to offset negative impacts caused by construction and development.

**Section 80,81** – Demolition Notice – notification given to the Local Authority that demolition works are to take place.

**SIP** – Structutal Insulated Panael – Timber frame

**SoW** - Schedule of Works – (see chapter)

**SMM** - Standard Method of Measurement - provides detailed information, classification tables and rules for measuring building works. SMM7 is typically used in the preparation of bills of quantities, and specifications in tender documentation, providing a uniform basis for measuring building works in order to facilitate industry wide consistency.

**SUDS** – Sustainable Drainage System

**TBC** – To Be Confirmed
**TF** – Timber Frame

**TFEE** – Target Fabric Energy Efficiency – part of the SAP calculation

**U Value** – see chapter

**UKTFA** - UK Timber Frame Association

**VAT** – Value Added Tax

**VCL** – Vapour Control Layer

# ABOUT THE AUTHOR

Vince Holden has over 45 years' experience in construction. He began his career from school with a local construction company that specialised in timber frame construction, obtaining an apprenticeship in carpentry and joinery, and then carrying on with education in site management and surveying. By the time he formed Holden Management Services to focus on Project Management in 2010, Vince's all-embracing experience had taken him through sub-contract carpentry, his own roofing company, and then on to wide-ranging construction and house building. His strong work ethos enabled him to maintain the exemplary status of A1 Zurich Registered Builder for 15 years.

Vince is passionate about and has many years of experience in the sustainability sector, working on renewable technology, energy efficiency, and related matters. He has worked on developing and proving new technologies, reducing energy costs and the environmental impact of buildings. His extensive knowledge of traditional and timber frame construction places him in a position to offer advice on the management of numerous methods of domestic system build.

In 2012, Vince Holden was accepted into the Chartered Institute of Building, qualifying as chartered member in 2016, then in 2018 became a chartered member of the Chartered Association of Building Engineers

Vince is married and blessed with a daughter and two sons. He lives with his wife, their two dogs, a parrot, and, at the time of writing, five ducks and ten chickens, in an old farmhouse in north Hampshire.

Printed in Poland
by Amazon Fulfillment
Poland Sp. z o.o., Wrocław

50947180R00167